To the wonderful churches I have served over the past 30 years of pastoral ministry:
- Westside Church—Newark, Ohio
- Malone Chapel—Tampa, Florida
- Heritage Memorial Church—Washington Court House, Ohio
- First Church of the Nazarene—Oklahoma City
- First Church of the Nazarene—Nashville

Thanks for everything; you have taught me about building God's Church. Thanks for the love and affirmation you gave to our family. Linda, Seth, and Adam join me in saying, "You are loved!"

STAN TOLER
Eph. 3:20-21

CONTENTS

Acknowledgments   7

Introduction   9

The Evaluation Principle
1. Diagnosis vs. Evaluation   11

The Leadership Principle
2. Leadership vs. Vision   31

The Lay Ministry Principle
3. Lay Ministry vs. Involved Laity   62

The Marketing Principle
4. Guilt-Driven Evangelism vs.
   Love-Motivated Outreach   84

The Assimilation Principle
5. Follow-up Discipleship vs. "Y'all Come Back!"   104

The Caring Principle
6. Traditional Pastoral Care vs. Intensive Care   120

The Giving Principle
7. Fund-raising vs. Generous Biblical Stewardship   130

The Celebration Principle
8. Worship vs. Celebration   139

Acknowledgments

Special thanks—

To Bob Brower and the Beacon Hill Press of Kansas City leadership team, which includes Michael Estep and Kelly Gallagher. Thank you for your continual commitment to building God's kingdom through print. You are loved!

To Jim Wilcox for the long hours you spent editing this project. You are a brother beloved!

To Mechelle Fain and Jim Williams for your creative and administrative support.

Introduction

Every church I have pastored has experienced marvelous growth. I am writing this book as I near the completion of 30 years of pastoral ministry. I have been privileged to serve five wonderful congregations and to serve on staff at Lancaster Faith Memorial Church with Tom Hermiz and John Maxwell.

Each ministry opportunity provided great and unique challenges. Each one brought tremendous joy as we watched God grow His church.

Often I am asked as I speak at ministers' retreats, conferences, and the INJOY Model Church workshops, "What is the secret to growing the church?"

My answer is simply this: As a young pastor I discovered the secret to church growth in principles that involve Spirit-producing-life applications versus flesh-producing-flesh programming!

In this book you will discover with me the eight principles that always succeed in building God's church.

First Pet. 1:22-25 reminds us that God's Word must be central to everything we do in the local church:

Now that you have purified yourselves by obeying the truth so that you have sincere love for your brothers, love one another deeply, from the heart. For you have been born again, not of perishable seed, but of imperishable, through the living and enduring word of God. For, "All men are like grass, and all their glory is like the flowers of the field; the grass withers and the flowers fall, but the word of the Lord stands forever." And this is the word that was preached to you.

Our responsibility is to sow the seed!

Additionally, James 5:7-8 reminds us of the need for patience in ministry. Thankfully, I was able to serve 10 years in a farming community with farmers as leaders on my church board. Through that experience I gained invaluable experience and patience! "Be patient, then, brothers, until the Lord's coming. See how the farmer waits for the land to yield its valuable crop and how patient he is for the autumn and spring rains. You too, be patient and stand firm, because the Lord's coming is near."

Another aspect of ministry that must not be forgotten is the reality of rewards in heaven someday. First Cor. 3:6-8 tells us that we should work for God's glory, not the rewards of man: "I planted the seed, Apollos watered it, but God made it grow. So neither he who plants nor he who waters is anything, but only God, who makes things grow. The man who plants and the man who waters have one purpose, and each will be rewarded according to his own labor."

Finally, the harvest principle of reproduction in Gen. 1:11 gives us insight into the importance of sowing the seed and watching as God grows His Church: "Then God said, 'Let the land produce vegetation: seed-bearing plants and trees on the land that bear fruit with seed in it, according to their various kinds.'"

God is growing His Church. It is my firm conviction that He uses willing and dedicated leaders to achieve this process. My prayer is that you will let God take your unique gifts and personality and mold you into a great pastor.

The Evaluation Principle

CHAPTER 1

DIAGNOSIS vs. EVALUATION

The Difference Between Going to a Doctor and Going to an Accountant

*Churches continue to offer the same old generic
programming to a society that is segmented
into a million different niches.*
—Rick Warren

THE PRINCIPLE OF DIAGNOSIS

How long has it been since you found yourself lying awake at 2:13 A.M., unable to figure out why your head was pounding, fretting over the *20/20* segment you watched earlier about the recent increase in brain tumors, worried that if you ever fell asleep you'd wake up in an ICU somewhere, staring up at a room full of masked strangers?

Perhaps you suffer with a nagging pain in the small of your back that goes away only if you lie perfectly still at a 9-degree angle for 17 minutes on your left side, get up and walk for 3.8 minutes, then lie down on your right side at a

11

2-degree angle for 15.2 minutes, eat a bowl of raisin bran, then take 3 ibuprofen tablets and a Bayer aspirin with a glass of ice water. You've listened to your nursing friend for the last 8 months, read 3 of the thickest medical journals you could buy, and watched every television talk show on lower back pain. Still, you have no clue how you'll ever find permanent relief.

At these moments in life you would give anything to find out what is causing your malady—and the desperation is so great, you wouldn't even care what the solution is, just so you could get some relief from the excruciating pain.

Five years ago my wife, Linda, was diagnosed with cancer. For a few weeks prior to her going to the doctor, she had noticed several things in her daily life that just didn't seem normal, but she kept thinking they would go away with time. Then the brief darts of pain commenced, but she passed them off as things that come with age or perhaps eating the wrong foods at the wrong times. Finally she decided she had been in pain for too long and made an appointment to see our doctor, who promptly sent her to a specialist. She was immediately scheduled for surgery as the tests all came back positive: colon cancer.

It was a Sunday evening when we checked into the hospital after our evening church service in Nashville, where we were pastoring. Dr. Santi, our doctor and surgeon, came by that night to visit with us and tell us about the procedure, possibilities, and plans. He took out a clipboard and a piece of paper and diagrammed her colon for us. He showed us exactly where the tumors were located and pointed out the large tumor on the X-ray that he had determined to be malignant. In great painstaking detail, he demonstrated how he was going to do the resectioning, how much of the colon would be removed, what complications he might experience, and possible prognoses. Linda and I did a lot of soul-searching and looking at each other's eyes that night as Dr. Santi spoke to us, wondering what the next day would bring and how drastically our lives might change.

When he finished, Dr. Santi did something I will never forget. "I am only a human being," he said. "I have to rely on God for everything I do." We had had no indication up to that moment that Dr. Santi was anything more than a great surgeon: now we knew he was a great Christian surgeon! What an instant comfort that was! He reached over and took Linda's hands and held them up toward heaven. "Lord," he began, "tomorrow our hands will be in Your hands, and we are going to trust Linda to Your care." He then prayed for me. As Dr. Santi left, Linda and I held each other's hands and thanked God for providing us with this marvelous Christian man as both a minister to her body and a pastor to our hearts.

Linda's surgery was a success. The surgical team had to do just about everything Dr. Santi had told us they might have to do; there were no surprises. She was placed in the intensive care unit until she stabilized and was then moved to a regular room for seven days until we took her home. Although it took several months for her energy to return and her routines to normalize, and there were many times when a sore spot on her leg or a pain in her arm caused us instant alarm, she has continued to get clean bills of health in the many checkups she has had since the surgery. Today she is teaching at an elementary school just three blocks from where we live and is as involved as ever in the lives of her family, friends, and church fellowship.

We praise God that He has healed Linda, but we are also glad we accepted the doctor's *diagnosis* and step-by-step *plan* for immediate action. Prov. 16:9 reminds us that "in his heart a man plans his course, but the LORD determines his steps." Planning is the design of hope for the future, whether the plans concern our physical health, our spiritual well-being, our families, our churches, our vocations, or even our vacations. It is in our planning that the strategies that bring success are made out, laid out, and paid out. Good planning is rarely an attempt to *predict* the future; it is more frequently an opportunity to *direct* the future. It proactively prepares the leader of a local church to shape and regulate growth.

THE CHURCH BECOMING PRAYERFULLY DIAGNOSTIC

Before any plans for church growth can survive (much less thrive), it is necessary to make an honest assessment of your local church situation. I recently became acquainted with Bobb Biehl, whose book *Boardroom Confidence* is one of my favorites. He teaches an acronym—DOCTOR— when he speaks about restructuring organizations and planning for church growth.

D IRECTION
O RGANIZATION
C ASH
T RACKING
O VERALL EVALUATION
R EFINEMENT

Source: Bobb Biehl

Just as all of us need a doctor now and then to help us stay physically or psychologically healthy, local churches would also benefit by having periodic checkups with Bobb Biehl's DOCTOR. His plan can provide a state-of-the-church report that will offer us insights as we make plans to direct the future of our congregations. There will be days when diagnosis is painful, sometimes excruciating. It's not pleasant to seek areas that need improvement, because improvement might mean changing personnel, policy, or practice. But when we face these realities honestly and begin to set the plan in order, down the road we will look back and say, "Praise the Lord. We are so glad we listened to the doctor."

Several years ago the perennial Super Bowl contenders, the Dallas Cowboys, looked at the direction the team seemed to be heading and began to assess the causes of its rather sudden and severe decline. As a result of their study, they decided it was time to recharge the batteries and make some drastic changes in the team. Out went the original ownership and its veteran coach, Tom Landry, and in came a man from Arkansas named Jerry Jones with his new coach, Jimmy Johnson. One of their first moves was to trade the Cowboys' marquis player, Herschel Walker, to another team for the rights to a series of draft choices over the next few years, wholeheartedly believing that suffering in the short term would reap huge benefits in the long run. How right they were! With those drafts they built a team that some have called "America's Team."

If you were to ask any of the people involved in the decisions of those transitional days whether those moments were easy, I daresay none of them would nod in affirmation. But if you were to ask those same people if those moments were worth what has since transpired, the response would have to be an enthusiastic display of championship rings.

Professional sports teams may call it rebuilding for the future, and corporate America might term it downsizing or restructuring or company merging. The medical community might simply refer to it as major surgery. But whatever the term, it all boils down to virtually the same principle: *diagnosing* the problem and developing a successful strategic plan for success. We'd be wise in the church to borrow some of that mind-set, I think, when we seek to build the kingdom of God.

A COMMITMENT TO YOUR PLACE OF SERVICE

Late great humorist Erma Bombeck wrote a book several years ago that has brought great joy to me over and over again. In the book she reports that the grass is not really greener on the other side of the fence where the Joneses live—it just *seems* that way because they own a defective septic tank. In other words, while it might appear on the surface that the Joneses have it all together and are producing the best crop of Bermuda this side of the Triangle, they've got some awful problems of their own.

As church builders, we must admit that every church has its problems; after all, every church is in reality a hospital full of sick people who need help. And we all know that when we are dealing with people, especially sick people, we're bound to face failure, shortcomings, and disappointments. So whether it's a need for more money to pay district budgets or a relational gap between Brother Smith and Sister Brown or a leaking roof with a defective air conditioner, all churches and pastors might be tempted to look over the fence in search of greener pastures. Statistics show that pastors change churches every 2.9 years on the average. That's not very long to diagnose and plan, not to mention implement and do. Let's face it—there's no growing a church without a *committed leadership team.*

Not long ago my friend Jim was telling me about his 16-year-old son who had just earned his driver's license and was feeling suddenly mature. On the way home from the Department of Motor Vehicles, Jim talked to his son about the responsibilities that accompany the privilege of driving: insurance, gas, maintenance, and so on.

"Now you realize, Ben," Jim began, "that our car insurance is going to double or triple, so we're expecting you to help us make up the difference by getting a job for the summer."

At that moment Ben was thinking only about driving

over to his friends' houses that day. "OK," he quickly replied.

Summer came, and true to his word, Ben indeed got a job with a lawn care service. What he began to realize after he started pushing a mower and hauling the edger, though, was that lawn duty in the summer can become unbearably hot work. Sure enough, it wasn't too long—about the seventh day—that he started grousing about how little pay he was getting for suffering so much physical stress. But if there's one thing my friend and his wife have modeled for their children over the years, it's the idea that once a job is started, you stick with it until it is finished. So even though Ben didn't like sweating bullets for pennies, he knew that if he quit on his first *real* job, the next one would be that much harder to stick to.

We can't afford to look for microwave-quick fixes to problem areas in the local church. It's far too easy in our throwaway, drive-through, convenience-store society to seek immediate remedies that hide rather than alleviate. If we're going to grow our churches and nurture them into the Kingdom, then we will have to be *committed* to whatever it takes to follow the will of God and stick to the job, even if it sometimes means sweating bullets for pennies.

STREAMLINING THE CHURCH ORGANIZATION

The Old Testament church was rigid in its control and long on its list of rules and regulations. Christians live under the New Testament covenant of God with a prevailing law of mercy, grace, and love. Yet many churches today have fallen into a hierarchical, militaristic approach to managing themselves. That is not a model for the 21st-century church. We must no longer feel that we have to control everything or everything will fall apart. People should feel our church system is friendly and relaxed so they will be willing to get involved in the process of building the kingdom of God. Effective leaders must learn more about team building, team concepts, and how to open up the church's organizational chart so that it is more user-friendly. The only way that can happen is if we make some profound changes and quit being churches that are institutions run by a bunch of control freaks.

In recent years there seems to have been a significant paradigm shift in church organization from single control centers to multiversities of ministries. This shift is most notable in the role of the pastor as his or her hands-on ministry decreases and the congregation's hands-on ministry increases. This trend is difficult for many pastors whose personalities tend to lead by quick decision and lots of action.

A second characteristic of this paradigm shift is that both the pastor's and the congregation's gifts become more clearly focused. William Easum has written a delightful book titled *Making Gourmet Burgers Out of Sacred Cows,* in which he contends that these churches are permission-giving churches. As the pastor confidently gives people permission to get involved, they become more focused on their gifts and are empowered to minister.

A third characteristic is that both the quality and the quantity of ministry increases. Pastors are becoming free to do more types of ministry and to do them with a higher degree of excellence because they have let more people get involved and have trained them to assume responsibility. Pastors are no longer one-man shows but have grown into visionaries, planners, and models of leadership and growth.

Fourth, there are often growth pains associated with this paradigm shift, because for some people traditions die hard, and the threat of change causes them to resist.

For instance, a restaurant near my home has big barrels of peanuts at the entrance so that if you're in line and have to wait for a table, you can stand there and snack (sometimes until you're too full to order a meal). They tell you it is perfectly acceptable to toss the shells onto the floor, and even when you're seated they give you a small bucket of peanuts. For a boy raised by a mother who made her children make their beds at the Holiday Inn ("No one is going to say we're dirty people!") you can imagine the problem. The first time I went to Logan's and saw those peanut shells on the floor, something in me said, "No way! My mother would not approve." So I piled my peanut shells onto the table in a neat stack. When our server came to the table, she shoved them to the floor and said, "We'll clean them up later."

That's the situation of the church today. Changes are occurring everywhere—and it's OK. The church bulletin, once a mimeographed symbol of stability and hope in the church, is now a worship folder produced on a computer. The narthex became the foyer became the vestibule became the lobby. Things are changing, and as a result we are going to look at things differently. This is not to say that we must change the way we believe. But we've got to gear up to the day in which we are living. Rick Warren, the pastor of Saddleback Community Church in Los Angeles, writes in his new book, *The Purpose-Driven Church*, that "churches continue to offer the same old generic programming to a society that is segmented into a million different niches." If the church is going to survive, it must keep up. And if it is going to grow, it must move out into the lead, onto the cutting edge.

There are five basic paradigms in the local churches in our country. First, there is the *witnessing church*. Its primary focus is outreach, which makes the primary role of the pastor that of an evangelist. The congregation's role is to "bring them in." Second, there is the *celebration church*, whose primary function is to lead the congregation in worship. The pastor, then, becomes a performer, and the congregation becomes his or her audience. Third, there is the *fellowshipping church*. These people are into fellowship in a big way. The pastor becomes a chaplain who goes to the hospitals every day and looks over the new names on the list to make sure he or she visits each one. Fourth, there is the *teaching church*, whose primary goal is edification. The pastor is the teacher, and the congregation is the student body. Finally, there is the *social action church*. This church is noted for its involvement in social ministries, and the pastor is a social reformer. The church focuses on the nega-

---

YOU MIGHT BE A PREACHER IF...

Your job description includes scraping pigeon droppings off the steeple.

Used with permission,
Stan Toler and Mark Hollingsworth,
"You Might Be a Preacher If . . ."
(Tulsa, Okla.: Albury Press, 1996).

tives in our society, battling abuse, violence, abortion, alcoholism, and so on.

Rick Warren claims that every church takes on one of these roles and is being reduced to a *life development church.* As with every area of the Christian life, balance is the key. We understand that it is all right to be a reformer, but not to the exclusion of winning souls. It's OK to raise both hands to praise Jesus, but if you're not teaching people anything and believers aren't being built up, you're out of balance. As churches learn balance, the pastor is free to become a leader/equipper and the people to become ministers.

One of the best methods by which a church can organize its leadership to rid itself of the sacred cow mentioned by William Easum is by finding the place where people best fit in the process of building the local church. After attending Florence Littauer's seminar several years ago, I began profiling my parishioners by personality type: sanguine, melancholy, choleric, and phlegmatic.

Sanguine people are popular because they deal with other people enthusiastically, are happy to help, tickled to tickle. They're excited to be there, wherever *there* might be, and they tend to do well in up-front positions, which makes them excellent worship leaders. Churches that show significant growth usually have at least one of these individuals involved in leading a significant portion of the service. What you must know in order to understand and work effectively with sanguine personalities is that they sometimes speak before they think, and they thrive on praise. They like new toys and love to have fun.

I love the story about George, who one day while talking to his wife blew his nose. After several good snorts, he folded his hanky right on the creases, again and again, until it was returned to its perfect square. He put it in his right hand and slid it down into his back pocket. His wife's mouth fell agape.

"Do you always fold your hanky like that after you blow your nose?" she asked.

"Yes—is that a problem?" George asked.

"Maybe," she said. "After 25 years of marriage, I had no idea you folded your hanky back up like that after blowing your nose."

"So?"

"So—I'm sorry to tell you that when I'm doing laundry and find your hanky neatly folded in your back pocket, I naturally assume it hasn't been used, and I simply put it back in your drawer without washing it."

Now George was stupefied. He thought for a minute, then said, "No wonder I always have so much trouble getting my glasses clean."

A second personality type is the *melancholy* individual. This is not a sad person, as the term often indicates, but rather one who keeps meticulous records and enjoys analyzing problems, occasionally losing himself or herself in deep thought. On the negative side, such an individual can be overly sensitive at times and get his or her feelings hurt easily. A melancholy person needs a lot of downtime when he or she can refuel.

One of my favorite stories is about a pastor who had been a child prodigy on the piano and loved music second only to God—at least it sometimes seemed that way. One Sunday he had a Christian opera singer visit his church, and he was so excited he could barely sit on the platform. So instead, when she got up to sing, he quietly joined his wife on the front pew. The beautiful music began, and the sanctuary was filled with the angelic voice. The pastor lost himself in the moment and lowered his head and shut his eyes. His wife nudged him a bit, afraid that the congregation and the singer would think he had fallen asleep out of boredom, and said, "Vernon, raise your head." Unfortunately, Rev. Vernon had left the mundane world of the sanctuary long ago and did not hear his wife's admonition correctly. So he raised his hand. His wife couldn't resist the opportunity. She nudged him again and said, "Raise it a little higher." He obeyed. She said another time, "Raise it a little higher." Now his hand was two feet in the air, fully extended, on the front row of the church. The opera singer, not used to such a response, stopped in mid-stanza and asked, "Sir, do you need to go to the bathroom?"

A third personality type is the *choleric*. These people are seemingly born to make decisions and take decisive action. They don't like to talk too much about this and that and the other thing. They want to get in there and do it. They are perfect for positions of strong leadership. Sometimes, however, because they are movers and shakers, they can be seen as overly objective and dispassionate.

Finally, there are the *phlegmatic* folks, who seem willing to do anything to keep the peace and be sure that everything moves in a calm yet efficient way. They are great for putting out fires that sometimes flare up in a church, and they work quite well with cholerics, because they tend to follow directions more naturally than give them.

Pollster George Gallup recently stated, "Fifty percent of the people in your church will not do anything, no matter what you ask of them!" He added, "Ten percent are doing the work of the ministry in most local churches. That's the bad news! The good news is, forty percent are just waiting to be asked!" Most phlegmatics need someone to invite them to serve on ministry action teams.

Several years ago the church I was pastoring had a phlegmatic as its treasurer. Every Sunday night he came to my office to count the money gathered in the day's offerings and said, "I'm not doing this another year. I love you, Pastor, but I'm not doing this another year. It's not for me." Over and over and over again—week in and week out. God's wisdom began to speak to me about another man in the church who would do a wonderful job as treasurer. He understood accounting, his disposition was perfect for the job, and I knew he would be happy to do it. But I didn't want to hurt the incumbent treasurer's feelings. One Sunday night as he began his litany of complaints, I asked him, "John, what do you really like to do?"

He answered, "I really like to work with my hands. I'm in the air-conditioning business, and I like to do those things. I believe I could do some things around the church, maybe fix water fountains and vents and stuff like that." So we made the change. Never had the church's mechanics worked better. And never had the church's books been neater and better balanced. All it took was a little honest conversation and a little human diagnosis.

PREPARATION AND PLANNING IS HARD WORK

A pastor was making conversation with a small boy before Wednesday night church activities. He asked the little boy about his age. The pastor inquired, "How old are you these days?" The little boy straightened and sorted four little fingers and answered, "I'm four." With genuine interest the pastor continued, "Are you going to have a birthday soon?" The lad replied, "Yep, and then I'll be five." A brief pause followed and then the boy announced, "When I'm five, I'll learn to share." Before the pastor could ponder the wisdom from the mouth of this "babe," the child added, "You know, it takes a long time to learn to share."

There is no quick or easy fix to any major problem that faces a local church. Often months of preparation and planning must precede the implementation of a solution.

Two types of planning that most have found successful are *inside planning* and *outside planning*. The former is sitting down with your group and working as a team in devising a plan or strategy. The latter is recognizing the need to call in an outside consultant to help get the ball rolling, through fund-raising, stewardship development, leadership training, or so on.

Before any concrete planning begins and certainly before any strategies are implemented, four questions need to be asked:

1. *Do I have complete knowledge of my mission?* (This means seeking input from those associates with whom I work closely on a regular basis, seeking prayerful guidance from the Holy Spirit, and spending time by myself to think, write, and read about my mission.)

2. *Do I understand my capabilities?* (What am I gifted to do, and where are my shortcomings? Who can I ask to follow me in my strengths, and who can I ask to take up the slack? Can I make a list of 10 things I do well and 10 areas in which I need help?) Some of our plans are so grandiose that we can't do them very well in a small church, and we need to understand that we have to take baby steps even in terms of planning the agenda.

3. *Do I have complete knowledge of my team's capabilities?* (Have I assessed their positives and negatives in an open way so that there will be no confusion as to what their roles will be? Do I have a team that complements itself and fills in gaps that might exist?)

4. *Do I receive constant feedback and have open communication?* (Some people speak out when they disagree or have suggestions, but others will not. Have I given those strong silent types opportunity to be a part of the team?)

As you diagnose and prepare to grow God's church, consider the following seven questions:

1. Who is our target group?
2. Do we have the right people in the right places to fulfill our strategic plans?
3. Do we need outside help with our planning?

4. Where are we going as a church?
5. Who will be responsible for what, and who will be responsible for whom?
6. Do we have the resources to accomplish our goals?
7. Do we effectively communicate the direction of the church?
8. How can we keep improving?

As you go through your strategic planning endeavors, you should do a review of what has happened every six months. Remember, most planning today is short-term by design. In the corporate world there are not many 10-year and 15-year plans, because the economics of society change so quickly. It is simply not feasible or cost-effective to plan in those terms. Planning 12 or 18 months at a time and assessing the successes and failures of the plan about three quarters of the way through it is a more effective strategy. At that time you can refine, hone, toss out, reinvent, and so on.

Several years ago I started using the following PLAN AHEAD acrostic to lead and monitor the planning process.

P REDETERMINE A COURSE OF ACTION
L AY OUT YOUR GOALS
A DJUST YOUR PRIORITIES
N OTIFY KEY PERSONS

A LLOW TIME FOR ACCEPTANCE
H EAD INTO ACTION
E XPECT PROBLEMS TO ARISE
A LWAYS POINT TO YOUR SUCCESSES
D AILY REVIEW YOUR PLAN

Remember that not everyone will jump onboard right away, so you must allow a sufficient amount of time for the plans to be considered and accepted. There is no universal time frame for all churches, but you should get positive or negative feedback within a couple of months. One of the great things about building a strategic plan is that if it goes well, the next year you can point to the successes and say, "God really honored this!"

CHURCH SIZE STRATEGIES

Lyle Schaller's book *Looking in the Mirror** provides the insights for the following diagram.

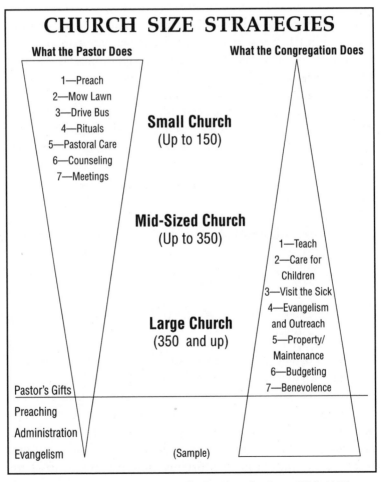

CHURCH SIZE STRATEGIES

What the Pastor Does

1—Preach
2—Mow Lawn
3—Drive Bus
4—Rituals
5—Pastoral Care
6—Counseling
7—Meetings

Small Church
(Up to 150)

Mid-Sized Church
(Up to 350)

Large Church
(350 and up)

Pastor's Gifts
Preaching
Administration
Evangelism

(Sample)

What the Congregation Does

1—Teach
2—Care for
   Children
3—Visit the Sick
4—Evangelism
   and Outreach
5—Property/
   Maintenance
6—Budgeting
7—Benevolence

*Lyle Schaller, *Looking in the Mirror* (Nashville: Abingdon Press, 1984), 14-37.

The *small church* that has up to 150 in regular attendance; the *mid-sized church* that has 151 to 350 attending, and the *large church* that has more than 351 in attendance. The average attendance in the churches of the United States today stands at 72, and the fastest-growing churches are led by bivocational pastors, those who work a job outside their pastorates. It is amazing what congregations of those churches of 10 expect their pastor to do. "Mow the lawn," some will suggest. "Clean the church—be the custodian." "Do hospital visits." "Preach good sermons." Even "Have all the keys to the church so that when we need one, we know where we can find one." The role of the pastor often defines the role of the congregation, so as a church moves through the stages from *small* to *mid* to *large*, the mind-set of that congregation must also change. That is very difficult, because sometimes we get a *large* church that has a *small church* mind-set, particularly when it comes to the pastor's job description. If the expectations are the same when the church gets large as they were when it was small, the church will level out the plateau in attendance, because a pastor or staff member can minister only so much. Once he or she is on all cylinders, doing everything he or she can do—that's it! You will never be able to hire enough personnel to get the job done.

The *small church* is often led by what I call "the grandma syndrome"—that is, an older woman (the matriarch) makes all the decisions. When she nods her head "Yes," everyone says, "Yes." When she shakes her head "No," everyone says, "No." The pastor is considered a worker or shepherd or caretaker, and it is his or her responsibility to make the church grow. The small church certainly has possibilities for growth in areas such as renewing a sense of mission and vision, starting small groups, involving newcomers, and networking evangelism opportunities. Unfortunately, this church is often fighting an uphill financial battle, and change is therefore resisted. Leadership is in-

Your job is never done.

Used with permission,
Stan Toler and Mark Hollingsworth,
"You Might Be a Preacher If . . ."
(Tulsa, Okla.: Albury Press, 1996).

grown, and the image of the church is that because it has always been small, it will remain so.

Most *mid-sized* churches have a leadership team that includes the pastor as the primary overseer of several lay-led committees. He is therefore viewed as the administrator or supervisor and has a small paid staff that includes at least a church secretary. Growth potential is high in some key ministries that could necessitate adding staff members, starting small-group projects, multiplying the usages of the facilities, and marketing the church. Some barriers that prevent this growth are inadequate buildings, an underlying unwillingness to change, poor staffing or planning, and limited resources.

The *large church* leadership is vested not only with a diverse pastoral staff but with trained laymen as well, which makes the senior pastor a vision caster, a planner, and a preacher. Its growth potential lies in communicating the vision of the congregation to the community through media, small groups that provide the intimacy necessary for growth, smooth operation, and evangelism. Poor assimilation of leadership or poor planning could cause the vision to get lost, and an inadequate structure could cause ineffectiveness in operating the church.

The primary enemy to church growth is clinging to tradition. This occurs when church leaders start living in the past rather than looking to the future. Lyle Schaller recently said, "Every day, seven churches in America close their doors and die." The only way to reverse this problem is to return to the vision for your church. When questions erupt—return to the vision. When doubts arise—return to the vision. When leaders stand opposite of one another—return to the vision. When attendance declines—return to the vision.

Not long ago comedian George Burns died at age 100. For years he had said, "I can't die—I'm booked until I'm 100!" But, with no more bookings, George Burns died. When churches run out of purpose, they die!

Dear Father,

Thank You for the opportunity we have to build Your kingdom, for the hope of heaven, and the faith we have for today. I pray that You will guide us in our planning for tomorrow's church, that we may continue to seek Your will and find Your provisions awaiting us in every decision we make. Be with us today, Lord, as we strive to be Your servant and spokesperson, ministering to the weak, feeding the hungry, and providing living water for the thirsty.

And now we ask for wisdom as we begin to make important decisions for our church, grace as we deal with other people, patience as we work through our shortcomings, and strength for the day. In Your name, amen.

CHAPTER 2

LEADERSHIP vs. VISION

*Visions are born of care and are given form and
substance through added preparation.*
—Paul S. Rees

THE LEADERSHIP PRINCIPLE

The first component we need to understand and begin
to assimilate into our work as church builders is leadership—that ability to influence. In Paul's second letter to his
spiritual apprentice, Timothy, he writes,

How I thank God for you, Timothy. I pray for you
every day, and many times during the long nights I beg
my God to bless you richly. He is my fathers' God, and
mine, and my only purpose in life is to please him. How
I long to see you again. How happy I would be, for I remember your tears as we left each other. I know how
much you trust the Lord, just as your mother Eunice and
your grandmother Lois do; and I feel sure you are still
trusting him as much as ever. This being so, I want to remind you to stir into flame the strength and boldness

31

that is in you, that entered into you when I laid my hands upon your head and blessed you. For the Holy Spirit, God's gift, does not want you to be afraid of people, but to be wise and strong, and to love them and enjoy being with them. If you will stir up this inner power, you will never be afraid to tell others about our Lord or to let them know that I am your friend even though I am here in jail for Christ's sake. You will be ready to suffer with me for the Lord, for he will give you strength in suffering. It is he who saved us and chose us for his holy work, not because we deserved it but because that was his plan long before the world began—to show his love and kindness to us through Christ.

And now he has made all of this plain to us by the coming of our Savior Jesus Christ, who broke the power of death and showed us the way of everlasting life through trusting him. And God has chosen me to be his missionary, to preach to the Gentiles and teach them. That is why I am suffering here in jail and I am certainly not ashamed of it, for I know the one in whom I trust, and I am sure that he is able to safely guard all that I have given him until the day of his return. Hold tightly to the pattern of truth I taught you, especially concerning the faith and love Christ Jesus offers you. Guard well the splendid, God-given ability you received as a gift from the Holy Spirit who lives within you. As you know, all the Christians who came here from Asia have deserted me; even Phygellus and Hermogenes are gone. May the Lord bless Onesiphorus and all his family because he visited me and encouraged me often. His visits revived me like a breath of fresh air, and he was never ashamed of my being in jail. In fact, when he came to Rome he searched everywhere trying to find me, and finally did (2 Tim. 1:3-17, TLB).

My early years in ministry were spent serving as John Maxwell's first staff member. I learned many leadership principles from John, unlocking the truth of the apostle Paul's admonitions.

Generally speaking, people tend to follow individuals who have an authority inherent in their *position.* This is the Maxwell's Level One of effective leadership. In rhetoric and persuasion, it's called an ethical argument. In other words, we tend to believe a president of a company or institution, a preacher, a commercial pitchman, or a parent, not necessarily because of what is being said, but because of *who is saying it.* Think about one of the last commercials you saw on television. Chances are it had Michael Jordan or Bill Cosby or some other celebrity in it, making you feel more secure that the product was worthy of not only your attention but also a piece of your pocketbook. "After all," you might have thought to yourself, "if it's good enough for Mike or Bill, it's certainly good enough for me."

Your congregation will follow you because they are supposed to: you're their pastor! Initially that can suffice, but as your pastorate wears on, it will become less and less healthful for your leadership to mire itself in this "have-to" mode. An effective leader is one who *pulls* his or her following—not pushes it, even though by nature most people who respect authority will support their pastor.

If you pastor one church and subsequently move to another, you will always start over at Level One leadership. I had been pastoring in Ohio for 10 years, and as a leader I moved through Maxwell's levels of leadership. But when I moved to Oklahoma City, I went back to Level One again, because they didn't know me. It didn't matter a whole lot to them what I had done in Ohio; I had to prove myself in Oklahoma City.

Maxwell's second level of effective leadership is *permission*—when the have-to of the preceding Level One evolves into the want-to stage of followership. This is the leadership level modeled for us by Jesus Christ himself, who called His disciples one by one to follow Him. Each immediately put aside his earthly plans and followed the Master.

A pastor-leader will gain this permission to direct and guide as he or she begins both learning how to follow God's leadership in his or her own life and teaching his or her congregation how to be effective followers as well. Now understand that followership is not blind acceptance, nor is it any sign of personal weakness; rather, followership is as important as leadership.

There are basically six characteristics involved in strong, powerful followership:

F AILURE

O RIGINALITY

L ISTENING

L EARNING

O BEDIENCE

W ILLINGNESS

Source: Jim Wilcox

First, a follower is not afraid to *fail.* Most successes in life are a result of failed attempts. Failure is the salt that seasons success. One university professor I know claims that a student whose grade point average is 3.97 has a far greater appreciation for success than a student with a perfect grade point average of 4.0. It is not until you have fallen that you realize how good it feels to stand up.

Being free to fail means that we must overcome real fears—the fear of being criticized and judged, the fear of being inadequate for the job, the fear of overdoing the job and losing all enthusiasm.

Second, an effective follower is an *original* thinker. When assigned a task by his or her leader, such a follower will not be content to do it the way it has always been done—he or she will think of a new method or means to accomplishing and completing the job. It may be as simple as changing the site for a meeting or class to a restaurant or nearby home. It could be a novel approach to fund-raising, selling used books donated by the congregation, or filling in for staff members on vacation. It might even be a church social at an airplane hangar, with live '40s music and World War II costumes.

Nurseries are frequently a good place to begin to think originally. First, that shag carpet has to go—it retains too many scents. That faded picture of Jesus that Grandma Stanley gave us has to go too. And take the chain off the door. Effective followers are innovative.

Third, a follower should learn how to *listen*. No one learns anything by talking or writing. All learning is done by listening and reading. Honest listening is a highly active endeavor, and for a nonlistener it can be a real strain. Taking notes, repeating key phrases or points, summarizing, and making eye-to-eye contact are all important components of listening. The most effective counseling is 90 percent listening and 10 percent advising.

Fourth, a good follower listens to the writer of Proverbs 3:5-6—"*Lean not* on your own understanding; in all your ways acknowledge him, and he will make your paths straight" (emphasis added). Following, then, is acknowledging areas of ignorance or weakness and seeking the wisdom of more experienced or better-trained people to fill in those gaps.

Fifth, a follower is one who *obeys* instruction. Sometimes the word "meekness" is misinterpreted as "weakness." This couldn't be farther from the truth, for only one who is secure and possesses a strong sense of integrity is capable of Christlike humility. Only one with a great deal of inward control can let go of outward control.

And finally, a good follower is *willing* to do whatever it takes to get the job done. It has been said that a person can accomplish much when he or she does not care who gets the credit. An individual is rich when he or she can do the assignments of the poor. One of my favorite illustrations is of a retired college professor, a man revered in the community and highly honored by his colleagues, who spent many days of his retirement on campus with a poker stick and a burlap sack, picking up the trash carelessly left by students—just to show them how much he loved them.

Maxwell's third level of effective leadership is *production*. People follow a leader because he or she has proven to be efficient and effective in setting and meeting goals for the local church. This is not bound to annual report information alone, though that is often an objective measurement of productivity. It can also mean spiritual camaraderie—a sense of goodwill among the fellowship, within both the community of believers and the surrounding community.

One of the dangers, of course, in this stage of leadership is workaholism and subsequent burnout. I've known many pastors who have put so much stress on themselves to do, do, do and then do some more for the kingdom of God that by age 30 they're out of the ministry altogether. It is a tragic danger inherent in the pastorate. Pastors should get a handle on this sense of overachievement early in their ministry. The best antidote to overdoing is delegating.

Level four is *people development*. This takes Wall Street's model of investment and turns it toward personal relationships. Here's Wall Street's model: give it $25 and forget about it. A teen is trying to go on a mission trip to Guatemala? Pledge $50 and be done with it. Conscience feeling a twinge of guilt now and then? Mail in $100 and celebrate with an evening out.

But investing in people is a donation of time, life's most precious commodity, and this takes strength of resolve and complete follow-through. It's more than merely networking yourself, for when you boil that down, it's a rather self-serving effort, isn't it? People development is definitely "them centered" and can be accomplished in many ways. Socializing—eating lunch with an individual or family, having a game night at your home, going fishing with a fisherman or bowling with a kingpin. Lay-building may include seminars on evangelism, Bible study, or family counseling; compassionate ministries; topical discussions and community courses.

I have "sons" and "daughters" in the ministry all over the world, and I know today that many of them would do just about anything I need, because we share the spirit of the Early Church of Acts. Developing people is sharing our strengths and our weaknesses.

Maxwell's final level of leadership is *personhood*. Unlike the initial stage of *position*, in which people follow you by virtue of your place in the fellowship, this idea centers around your integrity—who you are and what you represent. Billy Graham is still today named in the top five of the most admired people in the world, not because of his thick, wavy hair, but because of his integrity. There was a day, however, when I heard many preachers speak out against Mr. Graham, thundering from their pulpits, "Don't go near this man. He's a heretic." I once had an evangelist in my church use the King James Version of Revelation to do some kind of respelling of Dr. Graham's name in order to show he was the Antichrist. Yet today most of us quote him because over the years he has won more souls for Christ than any of us. The city of Charlotte, North Carolina, has named a busy parkway in honor of him. *Time* magazine has named him Man of the Year.

The spiritual leader is a *servant leader*, a New Testament model that certainly came to the forefront in the mid-'70s with the publication of Robert Greenleaf's book *Servant Leadership*. In it, Greenleaf suggests that churches do away with head tables, that pastors should shine the shoes of their people, go last in line, and defer all credit for goals accomplished. There is much to consider in those admonitions if we generalize them throughout all facets of our ministry.

The spiritual leader is also a *shepherd leader.* Luke tells us among the many miracles of Jesus—the feeding of the multitude, the conversation with Moses and Elijah, the healing of the demon-possessed boy—that Jesus said, "Anyone who wants to follow me must put aside his own desires and conveniences and carry his cross with him every day and *keep close to me!* Whoever loses his life for my sake will save it, but whoever insists on keeping his life will lose it; and what profit is there in gaining the whole world when it means forfeiting one's self? When I, the Messiah, come in my glory and in the glory of the Father and the holy angels, I will be ashamed then of all who are ashamed of me and my words now" (Luke 9:23-26, TLB).

And then in his second book, the stories of the acts of the Early Church, Luke quotes Paul: "Be sure that you feed and shepherd God's flock—his church, purchased with his blood—for the Holy Spirit is holding you responsible as overseers. I know full well that after I leave you, false teachers, like vicious wolves, will appear among you, not sparing the flock. Some of you yourselves will distort the truth in order to draw a following. Watch out!" (Acts 20:28-31, TLB).

Dear Brother Stan,

When you said, "Most pastors are chronically fatigued," I would have said "Amen!" but I was just too tired!
—Recent anonymous note at my seminar

H. B. London says in his book *Pastors at Risk* that 80 percent of all pastors fit into the chronically fatigued category of shepherd-leader. Most pastors are in this condition, he contends, from spending most of their time caring for people. "They don't get anything accomplished with the exception of caring for people all the time," he says.

The spiritual leader is also a *steward leader*, who has two responsibilities to live the mission of the Church and

---

You've ever written a letter of resignation on Monday morning.

Used with permission,
Stan Toler and Mark Hollingsworth,
"You Might Be a Preacher If . . ."
(Tulsa, Okla.: Albury Press, 1996).

to teach the stewardship of the gifts of God's people. The steward leader says, "I can combine the best qualities of the servant and shepherd leader and understand the mission, and my first responsibility will be holding people to the mission and beliefs." The term "stewardship" has too often been linked to money. But if I know that all the people of God are uniquely gifted, have distinct personalities, and at least one spiritual gift, then my real assignment as a spiritual leader is to get those people placed into ministry.

We learn to involve people in service as a steward leader rather than doing everything for them. If we do that first and foremost, God's Church will grow. George Barna said 40 percent of those who are in ministry today will be out by 2000 because they cannot keep up the pace. They drive by the church on Monday morning with their resignation in a brown paper bag weighted down with a little rock, throw it out the window, and shout, "I've had it!"

I remember one pastor in Chillicothe, Ohio, who wrote a note on Sunday morning to a church of about 500. The note read, "I bought a truck. I'm leaving to drive a truck. I hope you have a great time here. I'm gone." He just left the note on the podium. Now that's frustration! But the steward leader says he or she can do better than that; he or she can jealously guard the mission, the values, the beliefs, and can get people involved in ministry. Together they can grow God's Church.

I conducted a citywide crusade when I was only 16 years old. The first night I preached in East Side Church of the Nazarene. I stepped out in the vestibule that wasn't any bigger than a potting shed, and a man about 6'9" stuck his finger in my face. I suddenly realized how David must have felt in the shadow of mighty Goliath. "Kid," he bellowed, "you oughta quit right now! You have no business standing up here, telling adults or anyone else what to do! You need to go home to your mommy and not come back here tomorrow!" I learned the hard way that even Christians don't always appreciate what you're doing for Jesus.

I cried all the way home that night and got down on my knees. "God, oh, God—I'm quitting," I sobbed. But that night He assured me that *He* was not going to quit on *me*.

Effective time management can be a lifesaver for the busy pastor, a steward of God's time. I recommend three tests that I use to measure the value of a task when placed beside the amount of time it will take. The first is the test of necessity. How important is this errand, this little job, this project to the overall mission of this local church and my ministry? The second is the test of appropriateness. Is this what I should be doing at this moment, or am I simply delaying the inevitable difficult task I should be tackling today? The third is the test of efficiency. Is doing this task right now sensible, in the amount of time I have to give it—or am I going to have to do it over again tomorrow?

My personal priority list has three levels. Activities that fall into priority A are ones I must do. Sometimes these include family time. Priority B items are activities I should do. And in the last priority are activities that might be nice to do. But I have found that the biggest barriers to good time management are what I call time wasters. These include things like entertaining uninvited guests (assuming it's not an emergency situation), making or answering telephone calls, opening junk mail, attending countless meetings, and prolonged waiting. An efficient leader should be able to discern which people really need to be seen and in what order, which problems need to be addressed and in what order, and which projects need to be completed and in what order. He or she should precede each with a brief whisper of prayer. A good assistant is worth his or her weight in gold in this regard.

VISION BEGINNINGS

The vision begins with the church history. Every local church has a story to tell, and before the future can be seen clearly, the past must be understood fully. When I was pastor at Oklahoma City First Church of the Nazarene, one of my early projects was to write a document that we published about the 75-year history of that church. We included anecdotes, statistics, highlights, photographs, and testimonials. It provided the foundation for all that followed in our mission. Since then, the congregation has produced a state-of-the-art videotape that chronicles the moves and growth of their physical facilities.

The second step to developing the vision begins in the church leaders. In today's society you cannot simply walk to the pulpit and say, "I've heard from God, and this is the way it's going to be." You might hear someone shout back, "Well, you may have heard from God, but I didn't hear the same thing, Preacher!" Then you've got some real trouble brewing. If you want a vision to be caught by everyone, you have to share it with your leaders first, letting them fine-tune it and get behind it before you expose it to the entire congregation.

Third, the vision must always focus on the needs of others. You need to concentrate on your community and have a sense of awareness about what is going on. A local church that reaches only inward will become a maintenance shop instead of a healing hospital.

I'll never forget one board meeting at Oklahoma City First Church when we brainstormed ideas for reaching our community. One person said, "You know what I think our church needs? Flowers."

"Flowers?" I thought. "Give me a break!" But you can't say that in brainstorming sessions.

"This is one of the busiest intersections in the city," the man continued. "About 65,000 cars a day go past our church. We just look like the rest of these office buildings. We have poor signage, and there is nothing that says to these people when they are stopped in front of our church in a traffic jam that they are welcome here. There is nothing inviting them in. We need flowers to catch their attention."

The next day this man put his money where his mouth was and not only sent us his personal gardener but handed me a check for $3,000. Today when you pull up to that facility, it is breathtaking. People have actually turned into the driveway simply to take photographs of the place. They began to refer to us by saying, "Oh, yes—you're the church with all the flowers out front!"

Finally, the vision statement must include biblical priorities that connect to goals and strategies drawn up by the leadership. This statement ought to be brought before the congregation annually from the pulpit and followed up by a printed version in the annual church report.

Pastor Dan Walters of Tri-County Church in Hamilton, Ohio, after attending my model church seminar developed a strategic vision plan for that great church.

**When you focus
on basic needs,
you are always needed.
—Greyhound Bus advertisement**

A
G.R.E.A.T.
CHURCH

VISION
Grow through evangelism. (Luke 14:23)
Reproduce through discipleship. (Matt. 28:20)
Equip believers for works of service. (Eph. 4:12)
Assimilate new members into the local church. (1 Cor. 12:12)
Teach and proclaim God's Word in a relevant way. (Luke 9:60)

G	Goal:	To gain 70 new members by attracting 237 (5 per week) visitors to Tri-County Church (TCC) programs, activities, and worship.
	Strategies:	Direct mailings, seminars, concerts, personal invitation letters and cards, Friend Days, newspaper ads, radio spots, Sunday School promotion "All Aboard," Pastor's Welcome Class, Gift and Personality Discovery and Passion classes, Barnabas follow-up visitation, Andrew gospel proclamations, Timothy Discipleship assimilation, Abraham's prayer ministry, invitation program and winning souls through relations, and various methods of evangelism.
R	Goal:	To disciple 30 individuals in one-on-one discipleship.
	Strategies:	Timothy One-on-one; Three lessons for new believers; **Growing in Christ** (Navigators); Timothy II lessons for growing and mature Christians consisting of 20 lessons; Andrew Class on how to share your faith; mentoring one-to-one training; Sunday School class consisting of 8 to 12 New Life Study Lessons; New Christian class.
E	Goal:	To equip and train 89 percent of TCC regular attendees and active members for involvement in ministries, using their gifts and talents for Christ.
	Strategies:	Wednesday evening **Great Commission Ministries** and **L.I.F.E. Ministries.** Abraham—Prayer training, experience and outreach Barnabas—Encouragement, visitation, P.I.E. teams, Phone ministry called Keeping in Touch, Bakers of Men Team Andrew—Soul Winning Training Timothy—One-on-one Discipleship training for new and growing Christians C.A.R.E.—Sunday School caring ministry and Keeping in Touch and Christian Class
A	Goal:	To assimilate 45 new members into the Body of Christ at TCC (29 by profession of faith).
	Strategies:	Pastor's Welcome Class (every month). Relationship and Ministry is the theme. Gift and Personality Discovery class including a passion profile. Placement procedure will be according to profile results. The Assimilation classes (above) will consist of A New Outlook (vision), A New Beginning (Gospel proclamation), A New Communication (How to read the Bible), A New Family (membership with a ministry). Small groups, membership classes, and Sunday School Ministries.
T	Goal:	Teach and proclaim to the churched and unchurched the Word of God, and provide an atmosphere where worship and spiritual growth occur (in 90 A.M. and P.M. services and 50 midweek ministry nights).
	Strategies:	Sermons that are relevant and applicable; music and drama; concerts; seminars on special needs or our community; Sunday School, etc.

Tri-County Church of the Nazarene
Mission Statement
(with Vision, Goals, and Strategies)

OUR MISSION IS . . .

To fulfill the Great Commission by reaching the unchurched of the Tri-County area with the life-changing message of Jesus Christ.

OUR VISION IS TO BE A G.R.E.A.T. CHURCH . . .

G row through evangelism ....(Luke 14:23)

R eproduce through discipleship ....(Matt. 28:20)

E quip believers for works of service ....(Eph. 4:12)

A ssimilate new members into the local church ....(1 Cor. 12:12)

T each and proclaim God's Word in a relevant way ....(Luke 9:60)

A Great Commission + A Great Commitment =
A G.R.E.A.T. Church

Grow Through Evangelism

"Go out into the highways and along the hedges, and compel them to come in, that my house may be filled" (Luke 14:23, NASB).

Action words: going, inviting

Goals for 1994-95: Grow by evangelizing our surrounding communities with outreach evangelism, invitations to worship services, programs and activities where the love of Christ can be shared.

To gain 70 regular attenders by attracting 237 (average of 5 per week) visitors to Tri-County's worship services, programs, and activities.

Evangelism Implementation Strategies

1. Personal Evangelism Training
2. Relational Evangelism/Barnabas Bridge Building
3. Web Evangelism
4. Lifestyle Evangelism
5. Child Evangelism
6. Teen Evangelism
7. World Evangelism
8. Revivals
9. Sunday School Outreach Evangelism
10. Creating visitor flow for prospects through: direct mailing; seminars for felt needs; concerts; personal invitation cards and letters; Friend Day; Sunday School promotions; and media
11. Wednesday Evening Great Commission Ministries Weekly Evangelistic Services
12. Weekly Evangelistic Services
13. Sunday School C.A.R.E. Teams
14. Prayer—Abrahams

Reproduce Through Discipleship

"Take my yoke upon you and learn from Me" (Matt. 11:29a, NASB).

Action words:
discipleship, teaching,
learning

Reproduce disciples for Christ through one-on-one mentoring for new believers and growing Christians in the Word of God.

Goals for 1994-95:

To disciple 30 individual believers by one-on-one mentoring who will in turn reproduce themselves in the lives of others.

Discipleship
Implementation Strategies

1. Emphasize the importance of God's Word in their lives.

2. Emphasize one-on-one and group discipling—Timothy ministry.

3. Give training opportunities for equipping disciples.

4. Lessons on Assurance for New Christians.

5. Lessons on Christian Living for New Christians.

6. Basic Bible Studies.

7. New Life Studies.

8. Timothy One.

9. Timothy Two.

10. Basic Bible Studies for the Spirit-filled, Sanctified Life.

11. Basic Bible Studies for Children and Teens.

12. New Christian Class.

Equip Believers for Ministry

"For the equipping of the saints for the work of service, to the building up of the body of Christ" (Eph. 4:12, NASB).

**Action words:
equip, train, serve**

Equip believers for works of service, giving them opportunities to build up the Body of Christ through the use of their spiritual gifts, interests, skills, and abilities.

Goals for 1994-95:

To equip and train 89 percent of Tri-County's regular attenders and active members for involvement in the ministry of the church.

**Equipping
Implementation Strategies**

1. Offering training and equipping opportunities that will lend to the accomplishing of our corporate vision to be a Great Commission church

2. Training opportunities in Prayer, Visitation-Encouragement, Discipleship, Soul-Winning, and Assimilation—S.S. Care Team follow-up

3. Gift Discovery

4. Personality Profile

5. Interest and Skills Discovery that pertains to ministry

6. On-the-Job Training (OJT)

7. P.I.E. Teams (People In Evangelism who deliver love loaves to new visitors)

8. Bakers of Men (people who bake love loaves)

9. Keeping in Touch (phone ministry)

"Praising God, and having favor with all the people. And the Lord was adding to their numbers day by day those who were being saved" (Acts 2:47, NASB).

Assimilate New Members into the Body of Christ

Action words: assimilating, vision casting, membership, ministry, passion

Assimilate new members into the Body of Christ through relational ministry and creating a desire and passion in the heart to be part of a Great Commission church with a personal ministry.

Goals for 1994-95:

To assimilate 45 new regular attenders into the fellowship of TCC and receive into membership 29 of these by profession of faith.

Assimilation Implementation Strategies

1. Identify assimilation prospects.

2. Make effective follow-up on assimilation prospects—Barnabas Ministry.

3. Be nonthreatening yet persistent in follow-up.

4. Welcome Class to "cast" the vision of our church.

5. Welcome Class to help discover their gifts and passion.

6. One-on-one interview to discover how their gifts can be used in a ministry that matches their abilities.

7. Membership class.

8. Small groups.

9. Sunday School outreach ministries.

Teach and Preach God's Word in a Relevant Way

"And every day, in the temple and from house to house, they kept on teaching and preaching Jesus as Christ" (Acts 5:42, NASB).

Action words: teaching, preaching

Goals for 1994-95:

Teach and preach God's Word to the churched and the unchurched in a contemporary and relevant way, while preserving the message of salvation and holy living.

To make God's Word the focal point of our weekly worship service, with a strong emphasis on salvation for the lost and a holy lifestyle for the believers.

Teaching and Preaching Implementation Strategies

1. Teach, preach, and hold fast to the Apostle's Doctrine.

2. Preach evangelistically and give opportunities for response.

3. Create an atmosphere where spiritual worship has freedom.

4. Present the Word of God through weekly services, revivals, music, drama, Bible study, and Sunday School.

5. Mobilize the congregation for individual and corporate prayer, which undergirds all ministries.

Richard Meeks, senior pastor of Eastlawn Wesleyan Church in Indianapolis, recently wrote to me and shared how his church has experienced prolific growth by focusing on a basic need in his community:

OPERATION DUBARRY

It began in February of 1994. I was invited by Dr. Stan Toler to attend a *Model Church* seminar that he was leading here in Indianapolis. His invitation was in God's perfect timing. I had been pastoring Eastlawn about 18 months, and I was a bit anxious. I was asking God to give me a vision that would take us to the next level and beyond in ministry.

During the first day of the seminar, Stan used a short clip from the film *Sister Act* to illustrate the importance of vision and the motivation it provides for growth. As I watched the sisters bring people together to clean up their church and community, I began to pray. I wanted God to plant within me a vision for reaching our community, and I needed a tool to make it happen. My prayer was answered. God said, "Use the park!"

On my way home from the seminar that evening, I stopped at Dubarry Park. Immediately God planted within my heart a vision for this community and gave me a simple strategy to make it reality. The park was our key to the community!

The park was 40 acres of chaos and disaster. The grass was overgrown and needed to be cut. The picnic shelter was a shambles. The basketball and tennis courts couldn't be used because equipment needed repair. Gangs had polluted the pond and had painted the parking lot, picnic shelter, and playground equipment. The *Vice Lords* had taken over the place. However, I saw beyond the problems. I saw tremendous potential for a beautiful community gathering place.

It was time to take back the park! God was going to use Eastlawn to do it. As I walked around the 40 acres that had been neglected, I realized the park was simply a microcosm of the community. I began to put my vision on paper. We were going to reach our community by re-claiming the park. We would call it *Operation Dubarry.*

I continued to pray as I fine-tuned the plan. It was time to cast the vision. I took the plan to my D.R.E.A.M. Team (a team of personally recruited and trained lay pas-tors). This was something radically new to them and the Eastlawn congregation. My first task was to stretch the comfort zone of an ingrown congregation so they could catch the vision to reach their community. God helped me. They caught it!

Now I had to change Eastlawn's ministry mentality. The next few months were spent rethinking how we did ministry. We had to deal with our motives and our meth-ods. We had to decide who we wanted to reach, why we wanted to reach them, and what we were going to do to reach them. It was incredible. The more we developed the vision, the more motivated the people became as the momentum built.

Eastlawn decided to adopt Dubarry Park. It was now our mission to clean it up by enlisting the help of our neighbors. I called INDY Parks to get their permis-sion and blessing on this project. That's when I began to discover some of the obstacles we had to overcome to see this vision become reality.

INDY Parks didn't even know they had a park in our community. Those I talked with had never heard of Dubarry Park. They had to see it to believe it. I was told that someone would get back with me in a few days to discuss this adoption. Much to their amazement, they found the park. It was as bad as I had described to them. Since they weren't aware the park existed, it wasn't in their budget. That's why it was neglected.

Soon I was connected with the strategic marketing manager. It was her job to develop neighborhood cooper-ation with the department. She was thrilled with our de-sire to adopt the park and committed herself and her staff to helping us. We would become the pilot project of a new neighborhood parks program.

In cooperation with INDY Parks, we established a Neighborhood Beautification Day to clean up the park. In preparation, we scheduled a neighborhood meeting at the church. Armed with promotional flyers (provided by the parks department) we set out to canvass the community. Time for another startling discovery. We learned that most of our neighbors didn't know about the park. I could understand and accept their ignorance. After all, the parks department didn't know about Dubarry. What shocked me was their ignorance about Eastlawn. Many of our neighbors didn't know our church was in the community and that we wanted to minister to them. We had a serious identity crisis on our hands. My vision was confirmed. The park would become our entrance into the community!

We had our organizational meeting, and the attendance was great. The marketing manager from INDY Parks brought three people with her: the man responsible for park landscaping, the senior park planner, and the township administrator. Our neighbors were impressed with the team we had assembled to address their concerns about the park.

Within a few weeks, we had our Neighborhood Beautification Day. We painted the picnic shelter, swept the parking lot, dragged trash from the pond, repainted the playground equipment, and did other general odd jobs. It was terrific teamwork. Since our purpose was to promote Eastlawn while cleaning up the park, we made sure that everyone there from our congregation had a special T-shirt identifying them as church people. Many of our neighbors came to help us, and it was a great time to get acquainted. We also had television news coverage of the event, and I was interviewed and used in the story. The event was on a Saturday, so on Sunday night we showed a copy of the news story before the service.

What a confidence builder as the congregation watched Eastlawn on the news! They responded with applause.

Operation Dubarry was now well on its way. We continued having neighborhood meetings at the church to discuss plans for the park. During the meetings we would address the concerns for the park; then I would talk about Eastlawn's desire and ability to address the other issues associated with the neighborhood. We were gradually becoming a major force in the community.

Through the summer we continued making improvements on the park. Now it was time to move into phase two of the plan. We wanted to schedule some activities at the park that would demonstrate our desire to help the community. One of the great problems with the park was the fear the gangs brought to the neighborhood. We felt that if we would use the park, our presence could calm the fears and help drive out the gangs.

We scheduled a community picnic for a Sunday afternoon. After our morning service, we had a pitch-in picnic and invited our neighbors. It was fun, and everyone liked it. The first week of August we held our Kids' Camp in the park. Again we canvassed the community and invited our neighbors. We had 67 kids attend the camp, and we were excited. We followed Kids' Camp with Summerfest '94. This is a weekend event that features a hog roast under a big tent, along with organized games and activities for all ages. It was our intent to use the entire park. We wanted to show the community that we had taken back the park and they could come and use it. We were on their side, and they were beginning to notice it.

Things began to change. Dubarry Park has been totally refurbished. The city has updated the playground with all-new equipment. The tennis and basketball courts were resurfaced and restriped so people could once again use them. The picnic shelter has been replaced with a new structure. The pond is being cleaned. A new park ranger program has been implemented, using trained law enforcement personnel. It is now a place suitable for family use.

We concluded our initial *Operation Dubarry* thrust with a Friend Day. That Sunday morning we invited our friends from INDY Parks, along with the township administrator. We honored each one with a plaque, and I asked them to address the congregation. It was a great opportunity to build on our relationship.

A few weeks later, in October 1994, I received a telephone call from the Far Eastside Community Development Council (FESCDC). They had heard about our efforts with the park and the neighborhood, and now I was being invited to join their organization. I attended, and there I met a variety of business and community leaders. God had opened another door of opportunity for Eastlawn.

Within a few months, the FESCDC needed a place to meet. I offered our church, and they accepted the invitation. We did our best to be gracious hosts, and the community leaders were very grateful. They decided to make our Family Room their regular meeting place. Each month Eastlawn gets publicized as the meetings are promoted and the location is announced. The group has grown to become a vital force on the Indianapolis east side.

In May 1995 I was elected chairman of the FESCDC Steering Committee. This increased my exposure to community and business leaders. I've been asked to participate in a television program focused on community issues. I've been featured in newspapers and press releases. This had greatly increased the church's presence, because I am always introduced as the pastor of Eastlawn Wesleyan Church.

My involvement in the council has allowed the church to become a community center. If the group needs a place for a meeting, they call us. If the group needs a van to transport a group to a meeting, they call us. If the group needs help organizing a meeting or other event, they call us for assistance. Our influence is now being felt in this community.

The FESCDC has developed a newsletter that is mailed directly to 15,000 households. Eastlawn gets major coverage in the newsletter. We are included in all the announcements about the monthly meetings we host. We are asked to submit articles about what is happening with our building project and our youth programs. The community has come to appreciate our contributions.

In January 1996 a car in our neighborhood was firebombed in an act of retaliation. It happened after midnight on a Monday. Tuesday morning, as soon as the church office opened, the neighbors started calling us. They wanted to know what we could do to bring the neighborhood together and immediately respond to this violent act. Fortunately, we were able to use our community contacts to bring together some law enforcement authorities. We had a meeting with representatives from the Indianapolis Police Department and the Marion County Prosecutor's Office. It was a time to calm some fears and restore rational thinking to our community. As I was sitting in my office, God gave me this thought, "Eastlawn has come from being unknown in the community to being the first call. We are now a major, positive force for God and good." Praise the Lord!

We are now preparing to take *Operation Dubarry* to the next level. We have overcome our identity crisis and established ourselves as an integral member of the community. We have helped the neighbors successfully achieve a common goal and enhance our community. We have earned the respect of the people around us so that they look to us for guidance and assistance. We are ready.

Now our objective is to develop ministries that will give us an opportunity to share Christ by addressing the deeper issues. We are planning to provide educational support through day care, tutoring, and latchkey programs. We hope to work with the Gang Task Force and the D.A.R.E. program to educate parents and kids about gangs and drugs. We will be initiating recreational activities for kids, youth, and adults in our gymnasium. We would like to institute financial planning seminars to help our neighbors, since many are young two-income families. We will be using unconventional methods to take the message of hope in Christ to our community.

Operation Dubarry is a God-given vision that motivates Eastlawn Wesleyan Church to reach our community for Christ. We are embracing the dream!

How's that for vision?

Rev. Paul Moyer of the First Presbyterian Church in Broadalbin, New York, also wrote to me describing how his church reached out to its community to meet a basic need:

> When I arrived in Broadalbin, New York, in June 1975, one of my first tasks was to spend a year getting to know the congregation and the community. The First Presbyterian Church of Broadalbin initiated a community senior citizens group, which met at the church every other week. After attending your Model Church workshop with 10 of my key leaders, we developed a vision plan for ministry to senior citizens.

> First, we became a satellite for a countywide meals for seniors program administered by the county Office for the Aging. An emerging need for housing for seniors became evident. There were no subsidized housing opportunities for seniors who wanted to stay in the community but did not want to own and maintain homes. Our focus became exploring the options for the construction of subsidized housing for the elderly.

> I then discovered what in New York state is called a "rural preservation company," a delivery system for state and federal money to improve the housing stock in New York State. I joined the board of directors and began exploring funding sources for elderly housing.

> The board of directors of the rural preservation company allowed me to pursue this project. We began in

1992. Our first choice of funding was the Farmers' Home Administration 515 program. We considered applying for $750,000 to construct 17 one-bedroom units. The terms of the agreement were a repayment schedule of 1 percent interest and a repayment term of 50 years.

While we were exploring this option, we discovered that New York State funds a Housing Trust Fund. We conducted a market study of our area, which indicated that we would have little difficulty filling 40 apartments. We changed our focus and broadened our vision and applied to the New York State Housing Trust Fund for $2.4 million dollars to construct 41 units of elderly housing. (One apartment was set aside for the manager/onsite maintenance couple.)

A member of the congregation was willing to sell an 8.5-acre piece of property at a reduced value (because he believed in the project) for the apartments. He held the property for over four years while we engaged in the application process. There were many obstacles to overcome, which I will not discuss in detail here except to say that there were many days when we wondered if the project would ever come to pass.

We had to create a private water district to satisfy the Department of Health; create a state-of-the-art sewage treatment plant to satisfy the Department of Environmental Conservation; meet all of the requirements for placement of an elderly housing project in a rural setting, and convince the state that if we built it, we could fill it. Finally we overcame the obstacles and in 1992 began construction. The state was concerned, because this project is the largest elderly housing project funded by the New York State Housing Trust Fund in a rural area. Two months after construction was completed, the apartments were filled.

As I write this (May 1995) we have a waiting list of 40 and have been granted an additional $50,000 (by New York State) to prepare an application for $1.3 million dollars to construct an additional 24 units, to be funded by the New York State Housing Trust Fund.

As I reflect on the process this is what made it all possible:

- The full support of the church board and congregation
- A clear focus consistent with our vision of ministry
- A belief that this was part of God's plan for us

God gave us the vision; God would make it happen in God's way, in God's time. That belief carried us through many discouraging moments and seemingly insurmountable obstacles.

What a tremendous story of listening to God's vision and sharing it with a congregation of doers! Another illustration from the corporate world will help you understand the importance of visionary leadership.

After moving to Oklahoma City, I was impressed with a certain car dealership, so I bought a red Mustang convertible for my wife for her birthday. I arranged with the dealer to have a compact disc (CD) player installed. Additionally, my son, Seth, needed to have a used CD player installed in his car, and the dealer offered to install my son's CD player as well, free of charge. He sent me to a local Audiotronics car stereo shop.

I went to Audiotronics, where 45 minutes later Linda's CD player was installed. The next day I returned to have my son's CD player installed, and they were again very efficient. They took the vehicle around and began working on it. An hour and a half later a technician came out and said, "I hate to tell you this, but you have a problem with this stereo. Where did you buy it?"

I answered, "I bought it in Nashville."

"Oh, that's too bad," he said. "Do you have your receipt?"

I said, "I don't think I have the receipt. I don't know if

I could even find it in all the boxes we had when we moved back to the city."

He said, "Well, you better be looking for it."

Fortunately, Brad, the manager of the shop, overheard this conversation and came over to me and said, "Excuse me—I need to chat with our technician about this matter. But let me say this. If you will come back tomorrow, I will assure you that we will either fix this CD player, or we will give you one of ours to replace it."

I looked around and saw that their CD players were much nicer than the one I brought in, with prices starting around $500. I thought, "This can't be true!"

The next day I returned at the appointed time, and in 15 minutes they brought the keys to me and said, "The CD player is installed and working."

I said, "Let me ask you a question. Is it the one that belongs to my son?

"Yes," he answered. "It's yours."

I asked him how much I owed him for fixing it, and he answered, "Not a thing."

I asked, "How much do I owe you for installation?"

He answered, "Not a thing. That was in the deal with your wife's car."

I wanted to pay him something, but he said, "No, we agreed to do that. Let me show you what was wrong." It was just a matter of soldering some wires and fixing it—nothing to it!

"Brad, I want to ask you a question," I said. "Would you have really given me one of your stereos from your place of business that cost $500 more?"

He answered, "Absolutely!" He walked me over to where their vision statement hung on the wall, and he pointed to it and said, "This is what we are all about."

AUDIOTRONICS
Statement of Mission

To improve satisfaction through continual customer focus, resource development, and a structured quality system.

Vision Statement

To be a world-class supplier of high-quality automotive electronic products and services that provide superior customer satisfaction and value.

"We live by that statement," Brad said. He then added, "We didn't get to be in the top five Ford audio stores without living this statement out!"

Now let me ask you a question: if you put a sign out in front of your church that says, "The Church That Cares," then why won't you care? If the corporate world can fulfill this mission in the world, then the church must live out its mission!

The following diagram will give you new insight as to how mission, vision, goals, and strategies connect.

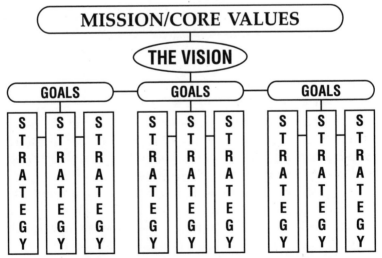

"Vision provides direction and goals shape the strategic plans."

—Stan Toler

LAY MINISTRY
VS.
INVOLVED LAITY

*Football is 22 people on the field who
desperately need rest and 22,000 people in
the stands who desperately need exercise.*
—Bud Wilkinson

THE LAY INVOLVEMENT PRINCIPLE

I recently overheard two mothers talking in the foyer of our church between Sunday School and the morning worship service. One of the mothers looked a bit frazzled and disheveled as she unloaded on her friend.

"I just can't get my kids to do anything around the house, so I end up having to do it all—the cleaning, the dishes, the laundry, the yardwork. I don't know how much longer I'm going to hold up. I'm exhausted."

The other woman looked her straight in the eye and

said a very profound thing to her friend. "Maybe you should just stop doing everything and see what happens."

The statistics on laymen who are actively participating in the ministry of the church are alarmingly lopsided. I have found that in most congregations, 20 percent of the people are doing 80 percent of the work, while the other 80 percent of the people are doing only 20 percent of the work. That may be attributed to the fact, according to George Barna, that 80 percent of ministers in America today are talking about lay ministry, but only 20 percent of them are actually providing their people with opportunities to get involved in ministry.

That's where the mother mentioned above had failed her children. Instead of asking and assigning tasks for her children—and then expecting them to follow through—she simply decided to do it all herself. We will become burned-out workaholics if we try to do everything that needs to be done all by ourselves; we will become effective leaders only if we delegate the work to those who surround us.

Laypeople should be inspired and empowered to fulfill their personal ministry in and through their local church and in the world; it is the responsibility of the clergy to enable and equip them. Lay ministry is not merely another program—it is a mind-set of the local church. And it is a primary biblical principle. Look at 2 Cor. 5:20—"We are therefore Christ's ambassadors, as though God were making his appeal through us. We implore you on God's behalf: Be reconciled to God." In his letter to the Ephesians, Paul writes, "For we are God's workmanship, created in Christ Jesus to do good works, which God prepared in advance for us to do" (2:10). And in 1 Pet. 2:5, 9, we are told, "You also, like living stones, are being built into a spiritual house to be a holy priesthood, offering spiritual sacrifices acceptable to God through Jesus Christ . . . you are a chosen people, a royal priesthood, a holy nation, a people belonging to God, that you may declare the praises of him who called you out of darkness into his wonderful light." All of these verses point out the importance of every believer's having a ministry in the family of God.

Every believer is gifted by God in unique and specific ways. Rom. 12:6-8 points out the importance of every member of the family of God: "We have different gifts, according to the grace given us," Paul tells us. "If a man's gift is prophesying, let him use it in proportion to his faith. If it is serving, let him serve; if it is teaching, let him teach; if it is encouraging, let him encourage; if it is contributing to the needs of others, let him give generously; if it is leadership, let him govern diligently; if it is showing mercy, let him do it cheerfully." As Reuben Welch said in his book by the same title, "We really do need each other." We need to say to one another, "With your gifts, we need you. You are unique, and God wants to use you in a specific, special way."

I once had a staff member who was quite sensitive to the leading of the Holy Spirit when it came to compassionate ministry. As the leader of 100 college students, he felt compelled to be their example of benevolence to the community around them, but he lost his balance along the way. One day he came to me, quite upset. "I don't know what to do," he began. "I've been thinking seriously about selling my house and cars and taking my wife and kids to the streets of the city to live among the homeless. I feel so guilty ministering to them only occasionally, then coming home to comfort and security at night."

I looked at him and said, "You have a certain gift of God, and that is teaching. You are a teacher." (He was also a full-time college professor.) "What your students need is someone to show them how to minister to the homeless of our city, not necessarily by selling everything you have, but by teaching them about the problem and the methods by which they can become ministers to the homeless." The relief registered on his face immediately. He simply needed affirmation in his calling.

Sometimes it's not a matter of refusal or even complacency. Sometimes the problem is ignorance or misdirection of the gifts. One of the significant roles of the pastor is to equip the laity for ministry. If a pastor is able to understand his or her congregation's spiritual gift mix and allow them to do what they are most passionate about, I think one of the areas in which he or she will spend much time is training people to do ministry in the Body of Christ. Workshops and seminars on teaching Sunday School, personal evangelism, writing, social services, and so on are a must when lay equipping becomes a part of local church ministry. In describing Jesus Christ and His relationship to His church, Paul says in Eph. 4:11-13, "It was he who gave some to be apostles, some to be prophets, some to be evangelists, and some to be pastors and teachers, to prepare God's people for works of service, so that the body of Christ may be built up until we all reach unity in the faith and in the knowledge of the Son of God and become mature, attaining to the whole measure of the fullness of Christ."

Recently I spoke at a church growth conference in Springdale, Arkansas. As I exited the church property, I noticed a sign reminding worship attenders "You are now entering the mission field."

The church should be both a place for ministry, *the church gathered*, as well as a base for ministry outside the church building, *the church scattered*. When we gather, we worship God, but when we scatter, we serve God. As you share lay ministry principles, it is critical that you talk about not only the gathering of the church for worship but also the scattering of the church to do ministry in the communities. We are all called to minister, no matter what our job description at work says. Some of the best evangelists in the kingdom of God have sat behind a desk or stood on an assembly line or bent under the hood of a car. Acts 2:42-44 reminds us that the Early Church "devoted themselves to the apostles' teaching and to the fellowship, to the breaking of bread and to prayer. Everyone was filled with awe, and many wonders and miraculous signs were done by the apostles. All the believers were together and had everything in common." We are becoming what Lyle Schaller calls a "seven-days-a-week church." It is not just this or that building we call the Church; it is we and they, the temples in whom God dwells, who are the Church.

Ministry is serving. It is love in action. Pastor Phil Bolerjack includes a ministry opportunity bulletin in the church worship folder. The bulletin lists the places and people in need of particular services that are available through that local church every week—from calling on the sick and homebound to painting a hallway to mowing lawns for vacationing members. There is no coercion or dictating—merely suggestions for service. By making the congregation aware of needs, the pastor is bridging and filling one of the real gaps in lay ministry: information.

MY SERVING COMMITMENT

☐ Yes, I would like to serve as indicated below

☐ No. Comment: _____

_____

_____

Card # _____ Phone _____

I have considered where I would like to serve at our church. I have recorded the ministry numbers for each service below.

Current Ministries		New Ministries	
# _____	# _____	# _____	# _____
# _____	# _____	# _____	# _____
# _____	# _____	# _____	# _____
_____ I am serving to capacity at this time.		_____ I am interested in receiving training that would enable me to serve.	

_____

Signature   Date

One of the hallmarks of the Church through the ages has been her willingness to serve. Her service has been evidenced through the worship of God and ministries directed toward fellow believers and to the world. We affirm that we as a part of the Body of Christ need to be recipients of grace. We also affirm that as recipients of grace we have a need to serve God through worship in all of its forms. Furthermore, we recognize the need to minister to the members of the Body of Christ and to reach out into our world as agents of change. The following listing represents some of the means available to us for the fulfillment of our obligations to worship and serve.

I. EDUCATIONAL

S—SUNDAY SCHOOL

The Sunday School is one of the primary arms of the church through which we provide learning experiences related to the Bible and living the victorious Christian life. It also provides a broad based support group for fellowship and need meeting.

ES AUDIOVISUAL SPECIALIST
ES2 TEACHER TRAINING SPECIALIST
ES3 PUBLICITY/PROMOTIONALS/BULLETIN BOARDS
ES4 SPECIAL EDUCATION INSTRUCTOR
ES4a HEARING IMPAIRED
ES4b ESL
ES4c NON-ENGLISH-SPEAKING (PLEASE SPECIFY THE LANGUAGE)
ES5 DEPARTMENTAL DIRECTOR
ES6 ADULT CLASS TEACHER
ES7 ADULT CLASS SUBSTITUTE TEACHER
ES8 TEEN CLASS TEACHER
ES9 TEEN CLASS SUBSTITUTE TEACHER
ES10 ELEMENTARY CHILDREN'S CLASS TEACHER
ES11 ELEMENTARY CHILDREN'S SUBSTITUTE TEACHER
ES12 ELEMENTARY CHILDREN'S CLASS HELPER
ES13 PRESCHOOL CHILDREN'S CLASS TEACHER
ES14 PRESCHOOL CHILDREN'S SUBSTITUTE TEACHER
ES15 PRESCHOOL CHILDREN'S CLASS HELPER
ES16 NURSERY CLASS TEACHER
ES17 NURSERY CLASS SUBSTITUTE TEACHER
ES18 NURSERY CLASS HELPER

C—CARAVAN

Caravan is a church-based scouting program designed for children through the sixth grade. Our Christian heritage is emphasized as are physical and social skills.

EC4 ELEMENTARY AGE HELPER
EC5 PRESCHOOL TEACHER
EC6 PRESCHOOL HELPER

CC—CHILDREN'S CHURCH

Children's church provides guided worship experiences for our children from preschool through elementary ages.

ECC1 ELEMENTARY TEACHER
ECC2 ELEMENTARY HELPER
ECC3 PRESCHOOL TEACHER
ECC4 PRESCHOOL HELPER

V—VACATION BIBLE SCHOOL/SUMMER CAMP

VBS provides intensified discipling of children during the summer break. Summer Camp provides long-term contact with children during the summer months.

EV1 VBS OR SUMMER CAMP DIRECTOR
EV2 ELEMENTARY TEACHER
EV3 ELEMENTARY HELPER
EV4 PRESCHOOL TEACHER
EV5 PRESCHOOL HELPER
EV6 CRAFTS DIRECTOR
EV7 CRAFTS HELPER
EV8 MUSIC DIRECTOR/HELPER
EV9 REFRESHMENTS
EV10 FIELD TRIPS/OUTINGS COORDINATOR

Q—QUIZ

The children's and teen quizzing programs launch their respective participants in intensified studies in the Bible that are primarily content related and serve as a foundation for the discipled life.

EQ1 TEEN QUIZ COACH
EQ2 TEEN QUIZ ASSISTANT COACH
EQ3 CHILDREN'S QUIZ COACH
EQ4 CHILDREN'S QUIZ ASSISTANT COACH

II. NAZARENE YOUTH INTERNATIONAL ACTIVITIES LEADERS

YL—YOUTH LEADERS

Youth leaders have the opportunity to give guidance to the youth of the church through some of their most formative years. The development of spiritual, social, mental, and physical skills is encouraged. The joys and fellowship in ministry to others as well as being ministered to is modeled.

YL1 CHOIR DIRECTOR
YL2 DRAMA DIRECTOR
YL3 PUPPET MINISTRY DIRECTOR
YL4 LIFEGUARDS—TEAM LEADERS
YL5 MISSION EDUCATION WORKERS
YL6 REFRESHMENTS HOSTS/HOSTESSES
YL7 ATHLETIC COACH

YP—TEEN PARTICIPANTS

Teens and young adults have the opportunity to be involved in meaningful and rewarding activities. Wide-ranging areas of service allow each teen to express himself or herself creatively.

YP1 SING IN CHOIR
YP2 ACT IN DRAMAS
YP3 PUPPET PERFORMANCE
YP4 CHOIR/DRAMA/PUPPET SUPPORT—STAGEHAND, SOUND, ETC.
YP5 MISSIONS PROJECTS/TRIPS
YP6 COMMUNITY SERVICE
YP7 ORGANIZED SPORT

III. DISCIPLING PROGRAM

The discipling ministries are threefold. One goal is the development of greater Christlikeness in the believer. A second goal is outreach. A third goal is the promotion of enhanced fellowship and service opportunities.

D1 PERSONAL EVANGELISM
D2 FOLLOW-UP ON VISITORS/ABSENTEES
D3 NEW CONVERT TRAINING
D4 HOST A HOME BIBLE STUDY
D5 LEAD A HOME BIBLE STUDY
D6 CONTACT NEW RESIDENTS

IV. MUSIC

I—INSTRUMENTAL MUSIC

The opportunity to worship and serve through the media of instrumental music is significant. Through the use of musical talents you help to set the tone of worship and/or response to the Holy Spirit.

IM1 PLAY THE PIANO
IM2 SUBSTITUTE PIANIST
IM3 PLAY THE ORGAN
IM4 SUBSTITUTE ORGANIST
IM5 INSTRUMENTAL FEATURES—SOLOS, ETC., PLEASE INDICATE INSTRUMENT(S)
IM6 DIRECT BAND/ORCHESTRA
IM7 PLAY IN BAND/ORCHESTRA

V—VOCAL MUSIC

Vocal musical presentations also help to set the tone for worship, including response to God. It serves as another means through which He may speak to us.

VM1 DIRECT CHOIR
VM2 SING IN CHOIR
VM3 ACT IN CHORAL DRAMAS
VM4 SING IN SMALL GROUPS
VM5 SING SOLOS

S—SPECIAL MUSICAL SERVICES

Special musical services may encompass a broad spectrum of both public and behind-the-scenes ministries that round out the musical/dramatic ministry of the church.

SM1 MUSICAL ARRANGEMENTS
SM2 DIRECT CHILDREN'S CHOIR/DRAMAS
SM3 MAINTAIN MUSICAL ARCHIVES
SM4 COSTUMING
SM5 PROPS/STAGING

V. FACILITIES/BUILDINGS

B—BUILDINGS

The condition of our facilities has much to say to our guests and visitors. A great ministry opportunity exists in the form of presenting the best possible appearance and comfort for those who choose to worship, serve, and fellowship with us.

FB1 GENERAL MAINTENANCE/REPAIR
FB2 SPECIALIZED MAINTENANCE—PLUMBING, ELECTRICAL, HVAC, ETC.
FB3 OPENING/SECURING BUILDINGS
FB4 KITCHEN SUPERVISOR
FB5 CUSTODIAL ASSISTANCE—ARRANGEMENT OF FURNISHINGS, ETC.

L—LAWNS

The external appearance of the facilities provides the first impression a visitor will receive of us and our commitment to God. There is an opportunity here to say "We care."

FL1 FLOWERBEDS
FL2 TRIM/PRUNE SHRUBS
FL3 CUTTING, EDGING GRASS, ETC.

VI. SUPPORT SERVICES

PS—PERSONAL SERVICES

The need to favorably greet and serve the needs of the congregation and visitors is a significant ministry opportunity. A spirit of warmth and sincerity is highly desirable.

SPS1 GREETERS
SPS2 USHERS
SPS3 PRAYER CHAIN
SPS4 PARKING ATTENDANTS

PP—PUBLICITY AND PROMOTION

The use of creative abilities to promote the events of the church provides an excellent opportunity to serve.

SPP1 BULLETIN BOARD
SPP2 PRODUCTION OF POSTERS, FLYERS, ETC.

TS—TECHNICAL SERVICE

The technologically oriented church of modern days requires skilled services to maintain its efficiency. Herein lies specialized opportunities for service of a technical nature.

STC1 OPERATION OF AUDIOVISUALS
STC2 MAINTENANCE OF AUDIOVISUALS
STC3 COMPUTER SUPPORT—HARDWARE
STC4 COMPUTER SUPPORT—SOFTWARE
STC5 PHOTOGRAPHIC ART
STC6 VIDEO ARTS
STC7 VEHICULAR MAINTENANCE

AA—ADMINISTRATIVE ASSISTANCE

People and office skills may require special talents that may be shared for the more efficient operation of the church.

SAA1 SECRETARIAL/CLERICAL ASSISTANCE
SAA2 OPERATE OFFICE MACHINES
SAA3 ASSIST IN SPECIAL MAILINGS, PHONING, ETC.
SAA4 MAINTENANCE OF LIBRARY

D—DECORATIONS

Through the use of God-given talents and acquired skills it is possible to increase the appeal of the facilities and create a warm or thematic environment for fellowship, education, and worship.

SD1 FLORAL ARRANGEMENT
SD2 DECORATIONS FOR SPECIAL EVENTS
SD3 INTERIOR DESIGNS/FURNISHINGS

FOLLOW YOUR HEART, DO YOUR PART!

There is a place for you at Regency Park! This guide is an overview of the most prominent ministries in progress. For more detailed information, please fill out a "ministries opportunities" card and place in the offering or the church office and a representative will contact you. Our Lord has blessed us with many opportunities for ministry, worship, and praise, and the methods listed within this brochure are by no means exclusive. If you have special talents or interests outside of this listing, please indicate them on your card. Remember, the fields are white, but the workers are few.

Regency Park Church of the Nazarene

The Church will not fully accomplish its mission in the world until laypersons are mobilized to find and fulfill their ministry. Not only is this a commission from Christ as He prepared to ascend to heaven after His resurrection, but also Paul says this throughout his letters to various churches. To the Corinthians he writes, "The body is a unit, though it is made up of many parts; and though all its parts are many, they form one body. . . . in fact God has arranged the parts in the body, every one of them, just as he wanted them to be. . . . Now you are the body of Christ, and each one of you is a part of it" (1 Cor. 12:12, 18, 27). And to the church at Rome he writes, "Just as each of us has one body with many members, and these members do not all have the same function, so in Christ we who are many form one body, and each member belongs to all the others" (Rom. 12:4-5).

Have you ever tried to worship at the Church of the Valley of Dry Bones? The services are so dull they couldn't cut butter, because there is no life, no breath, no spirit. Why? Because there is no ministry going on—just maintenance. In a maintenance organization, the pastor serves the 80 percent of "dry bones" and is a worker instead of a leader. The other 20 percent of the laity are doing the work.

The prophet Ezekiel found himself mired at the Church of the Valley of Dry Bones in the 37th chapter of his Old Testament book.

> The hand of the LORD was upon me, and he brought me out by the Spirit of the LORD and set me in the middle of a valley; it was full of bones. He led me back and forth among them, and I saw a great many bones on the floor of the valley, bones that were very dry. He asked me, "Son of man, can these bones live?"
>
> I said, "O Sovereign LORD, you alone know."
>
> Then he said to me, "Prophesy to these bones and say to them, 'Dry bones, hear the word of the LORD! This is what the Sovereign LORD says to these bones: I will make breath enter you, and you will come to life. I will attach tendons to you and make flesh come upon you

and cover you with skin; I will put breath in you, and you will come to life. Then you will know that I am the LORD'" *(Ezek. 37:1-6).*

And Ezekiel did as he was told, and the Lord did as He had promised.

Then the Lord said to Ezekiel, "These bones are the whole house of Israel. They say, 'Our bones are dried up and our hope is gone . . . I am going to open your graves and bring you up from them . . . back to the land of Israel. . . . I will put my Spirit in you and you will live" (Ezek. 37:11-12, 14).

Not long ago a pastor attending one of my workshops created a humorous vision plan for the Big Ol' Pig Church. He calls the folks who come to worship but not to work or serve spiritual porkers. They sit around, getting fatter and fatter, gaining pound after pound, but they're not growing.

BIG OL' PIG CHURCH

Our Mission Is . . .
To ignore the Great Commission (and a few lesser ones) and to do exactly what we want, the way we want, without thought to what could be or who might come . . . simply because . . . We don't care!
"Come, and be chased away"

Our Vision Is . . .
Being eternally the same
Inviting no one
Gaining nothing

Offering nothing
Loving no one

Putting down the lost
Intentionally not caring
Graciously letting the
world go to hell

At every Olympics I sit in my recliner, absolutely impressed with the various physiques on the athletes. I watch in awe as the marathoners carry their virtual skin and bones through the streets of the host city at a speed I only dream about. Then I see the weightlifting behemoths stride up to the bar and hoist the equivalent of a compact car above their heads. And then I begin to smile as I imagine the weight lifters trying to lift the bar with no weights on it at all, much less 500 or 600 pounds. At that moment I realize that fitness applies to task, and even though one person may be as thin as a rail and another as broad as a house, the thing that unites them both is that they are fit—not fat.

I think we can make a spiritual application to that. One layman may be fit for a certain job, while another with a completely different spiritual and psychological makeup may be fit for another, but the thing they have in common is that they are not spiritual porkers. They are active and fit.

In a growing organization, the pastor equips the 20 percent 80 percent of the time. He or she is a leader—training the people who have been involved in everything. Such a pastor knows that leadership is influence, so he or she finds the people who are able to influence others. Then he or she serves the other 80 percent of the people 20 percent of the time. This pastor is a modeler. Instead of running milk routes, putting a bottle into a screaming mouth, burping babies and changing diapers, all of a sudden he or she begins to minister to people who can in turn minister to others. The church becomes a place of participants—partners in ministry, rather than an arena of spectators. In a growing church the pastor and lay leaders together cast the vision. The lay leaders recruit and train others to lead, who in turn recruit and train participants, who perform the ministry.

Consider taking time to list the names of people you consider to be your "20 percent" workforce. What are their specific and special gifts? After you have done that, consider what steps you might take to disciple and train them, so that they in turn can disciple and train the other "80 percent." Sound simple? It's a long and difficult job. Seek God's guidance and blessing when your lay leadership buys into the principle; you will begin to see results within months.

RESTRUCTURING FOR GROWTH

Jesus taught us that we cannot pour new wine into old wineskins, lest they break. An old wineskin is dry and brittle, completely unable to stretch and expand under the pressure of being filled up. Most churches today are like old wineskins, structured according to the military hierarchy we instituted after World War II. It has relatively little to do with spirituality; it has more to do with immediate results and instant efficiency.

On the other hand, church structure does not cause growth any more than a hot oven will cause a German chocolate cake. What structure does is control the rate and limit of your church growth by providing adequate foundation. One way to measure the adequacy of your church structure is to look at its numbers. If your church growth has been leveled off for five years, you probably don't have the structure in place that allows growth to take place. There are many reasons for attendance to stagnate: overreliance on tradition, inability to adjust focus, lack of innovation, same lay leadership year after year, and so on. Another symptom of an inadequate structure is internal conflict. I have told every congregation I've ever pastored (some more than others) that I am not a fighter. If they want to fight me on every suggestion I make, every step I take, then they ought to seek another pastor, because I will certainly be seeking another church. A fellowship that bickers, fusses, argues, and disagrees about everything that comes along is not a fellowship that fosters confidence in its visitors. Growth in such a church is impossible. The third symptom of a poor structure is a discouraged leadership. If your church board, Sunday School staff, or volunteer base seems to be swimming upstream and losing ground, then chances are that the foundation is crumbling around them. They simply need better footing. When we restructure, we are saying, "Yes, we want to open up our system for more involvement."

Four elements of renewal are imperative as you begin to think about restructuring your local church. They are listed in chronological order, the first prerequisite for the second, and so on. First, there must be a time of *personal renewal*—when you get alone with God and experience an old-fashioned revival in your heart. This might be for as short as an hour or as long as two weeks. I have been known to crawl under my desk and pray until I felt I had touched the hem of His garment. I have taken much-needed retreats to a lake or to a mountain cabin, seeking His guidance and wisdom in major decisions. Just like going out on a date with my wife—talking and listening, which renews my relationship with her—so, too, going on a "prayer date" with my God renews my relationship with Him.

An article appeared in *Newsweek* several years ago titled "We're Too Busy for Ideas." The writer told about her first encounter with a Walkman. After about two weeks of wearing it on her morning and evening walks and bike rides, she began to realize that she was running out of good ideas at work. In her effort to fill her mind with music and conversation, she had emptied it of brainstorming and imagining. And so she stopped wearing the Walkman. She concluded the article by suggesting that in its attempt to bombard every waking minute with stimuli and noise, society was depriving itself of time alone. "Dead time," she wrote, "is never wasted time."

Pastors seem particularly vulnerable to this social philosophy. Sometimes a long walk alone in the afternoon can be much more productive in the long run than four hours of sermon preparation or hospital calling. Often a week in the woods will bring benefits for a year. Schedule into your calendar "dead time."

Second, there is a need for *corporate renewal.* This occurs when what happens to you during your personal renewal becomes contagious, and the whole church gets fired up, absolutely excited for God. One of my favorite teachers taught a subject many of us detest—English grammar. I mean, who cares if my participle dangles completely off the page or my syntax needs to be repealed? What made this class enjoyable was her enthusiasm for English grammar. She honestly loved the study of our language, from its parts of speech to its exceptional number of exceptions. When she breezed into the room, the class came alive. As she joked about what she had just heard in the hall or read in her office, we became aware of how fun grammar could be. I learned a lot about writing from her, despite my reluctance and reservations. That's what can happen to the body of the church when its leader comes into the sanctuary, exuberant and head-to-toe excited about his or her vision and mission.

Third, there must be a time of *functional renewal.* This is best described as prayerful diagnosis. What operations of the church contribute to its spiritual health and vitality? Which ones seem to miss that mark? Which programs count for eternity, and which ones seem to fill an insignificant need to appear busy? What is the primary need in the immediate community, and how are we adjusting our vision to address that need? What ministry would distinguish us from the other 20 churches in the area?

Finally, there must be *structural renewal.* This is where you begin to examine everything you do structurally. *A church can never grow beyond the dimensions of its base.* This has to do with property, your parking lot, your facilities, as well as your organizational structure. Visualize an eight-foot-long table. Now imagine putting sand onto the table, knowing that as the pile gets higher, it will form a pyramid that may begin to run off the sides. What can you do about that? Unfortunately, some pastors wouldn't do anything about it, but if you want the pyramid to grow and increase, you'll have to stop the sand from running off the table. If you don't make the base of the table larger structurally, you will discover that you cannot expand or grow the pyramid beyond the dimensions of the base. That principle is certainly true as well with church growth. If you have not laid a foundation or structure that is large enough, ultimately it will strangle and limit the rate and size of your growth.

Equally, *a church can never grow beyond its ability to care for a predetermined number of people.* Let's say your church runs 50 in attendance, and it takes one usher every Sunday to make your church hum. If your church begins to grow and soon you have 100, how many ushers will you need to continue to hum? You'll need two, won't you? Then why do so many churches continue to use one? Tradition and lack of vision—that's why. If you're wise, you'd have two ushers for 50 people and four for 100. Before I ever got to 100, I'd probably want to have four ushers: after all, I always want to be ready for company.

Not long ago I went to a church where children greeted people at the door. They were running thousands in attendance! Another church near one I pastored sent men in black suits and black ties to the street corners to preach every Sunday night after church, and they had their sons stand with them, also wearing black suits and ties. They are bringing up a whole new generation of church leaders. Many pastors complain that they can't get people into their churches, but if they enlarged the structure, people would be drawn in.

Rick Warren says that the nature of the church determines the structure, and first and foremost, *the church is a fellowship*. The number one reason people attend your church is for fellowship. Nothing is more comforting in life than to see familiar faces and friendly people, and I think that's one reason churches should have some kind of celebration at least once a month: a dinner together, a birthday party, a picnic, an anniversary, whatever. Second, *the church is a family*. This is based on Eph. 4: the church should operate on the basis of relationships, not rules. What has happened in most denominations today is that we have moved toward legislating everything with a "I so move" and a "I second that." Eventually, we will lose our vision and vitality if *Roberts' Rules of Order* usurps Christ's command to love God and one another. Third, *the church is a body*. And because it is a body, then it should operate on the basis of spiritual gifts, everyone pitching in according to his or her talents, desires, and needs. Finally, *the church is a flock*. It should operate on the basis of pastoral care and shepherding. When we structure our local church, we cannot ignore the care of the people. Unfortunately, too many are mired in traditional pastoral care, in which the church hires someone to run around and care for needy sisters and brothers instead of giving laypeople an opportunity to minister sincerely day in and day out. No one should be neglected in the Body of Christ. The church is a flock, and the pastor is its overseer. Pastors and lay leaders become facilitators of care for the flock.

Trends in church administration are certainly evolving too fast for many churches to keep up. Whereas we once structured under the committee system, we now have ministry action teams. Programs have given way to visions, and volunteers have become paid professionals. We have moved from slide projectors and ditto machines to big-screen televisions and massive duplicating machines. From typewriters to computers. From rigid rules to flexibility. As technology has changed, so has the need for identification of the church mission. Where are you and your church going? Where should you be going? Why should you be going there? To those ends the pastor today must establish a ministry action team to focus on restructuring by charting the church organization as it presently exists, circulating its flowchart that is open to newcomers, and reevaluating annually. The pastor should have a personal, professional, and corporate growth plan and will allow for management and evaluation, as well as definitions of major areas of responsibilities that establish lines of authority, accountability, and empowerment.

The following diagrams reflect a systems approach for leading the 21st-century church.

Where success is concerned, people are not measured in inches or pounds, or college degrees, or family background. They are measured by the size of their thinking. How big we think determines the size of our accomplishments.
—David Schwartz*

*From Stan Toler, Minute Motivators (Kansas City: Beacon Hill Press of Kansas City, 1996), 16.

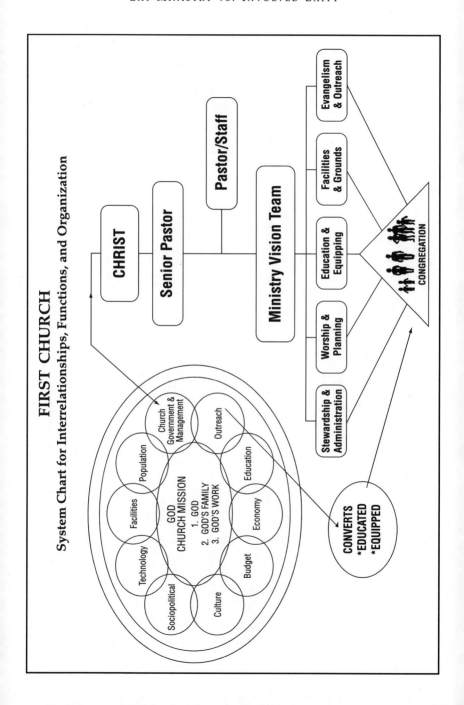

FIRST CHURCH
System Chart for Interrelationships, Functions, and Organization

CHRIST

Senior Pastor

Pastor/Staff

Ministry Vision Team

Stewardship & Administration

Worship & Planning

Education & Equipping

Facilities & Grounds

Evangelism & Outreach

CONGREGATION

GOD
CHURCH MISSION
1. GOD
2. GOD'S FAMILY
3. GOD'S WORK

Church Government & Management

Population

Facilities

Technology

Sociopolitical

Culture

Budget

Economy

Education

Outreach

CONVERTS
*EDUCATED
*EQUIPPED

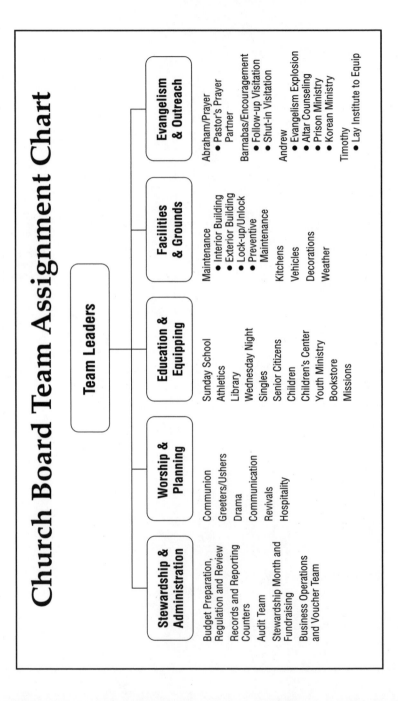

Church Board Team Assignment Chart

Team Leaders

Stewardship & Administration

Budget Preparation, Regulation and Review
Records and Reporting
Counters
Audit Team
Stewardship Month and Fundraising
Business Operations and Voucher Team

Worship & Planning

Communion
Greeters/Ushers
Drama
Communication
Revivals
Hospitality

Education & Equipping

Sunday School
Athletics
Library
Wednesday Night
Singles
Senior Citizens
Children
Children's Center
Youth Ministry
Bookstore
Missions

Facilities & Grounds

Maintenance
  • Interior Building
  • Exterior Building
  • Lock-up/Unlock
  • Preventive Maintenance
Kitchens
Vehicles
Decorations
Weather

Evangelism & Outreach

Abraham/Prayer
  • Pastor's Prayer Partner

Barnabas/Encouragement
  • Follow-up Visitation
  • Shut-in Visitation

Andrew
  • Evangelism Explosion
  • Altar Counseling
  • Prison Ministry
  • Korean Ministry

Timothy
  • Lay Institute to Equip

FIRST CHURCH RIG'S PROGRAM

Stewardship Month Team Leader

Church Year 1995

Indicators

Responsibilities	Goals	July	Aug.	Sept.	Oct.	Nov.	Dec.	Jan.	Feb.	Mar.	Apr.	May	June
App. (M.A.T.) with Pastor	N/A				✓	✓	✓	✓					
Select a Theme	N/A				✓								
Order Envelopes	250					✓							
Prepare Stewardship Letters	250					✓							
Commitment Cards	250					✓							
Partnership with God	250						✓						
Weekly Handouts	250						✓	✓					
Stewardship Testimonies	4						✓	✓					
Family Giving Units	10							(11) ✓PTL					

CHAPTER 4

GUILT-DRIVEN EVANGELISM VS. LOVE-MOTIVATED OUTREACH

*When you ask someone, "Would you like to be
a Christian?" what she actually hears you
saying is "Would you like to be like me?"*
—Stephen Fletcher

THE PRINCIPLE OF MARKETING

Christmas is one of my favorite times of the year—
streets are illuminated by a thousand lights, houses smell
like mountain pine, boxes are wrapped in glittering paper,
and the noels permeate the air. It just makes me feel good
all over. Sometimes, though, I feel pressure to give gifts—
too much pressure.

A friend of mine told me about such a Christmas several years ago when he was in seminary and quite poor. He
had barely scraped enough coins together to buy his only

brother a pair of boxer shorts for Christmas. Feeling that his meager gift wouldn't look all that bountiful in front of his family on Christmas morning, he also folded neatly into the box a couple of ties he no longer wore. "There," he thought. "That oughta do it."

Christmas morning came. His brother, who had already started a teaching career and had plenty of money for the first time in his life, enough to keep his refrigerator full of Coca-Cola, placed his gift in my friend's lap. Opening it, he was aghast to find a beautiful, expensive sweater worth 20 or 30 times what he had spent on those silly boxer shorts.

Then it was his brother's turn. "Wow!" his brother exclaimed. "I love boxer shorts! And these ties will go perfectly with my suit. Thanks."

That's the way it is with God's gift of grace and mercy. Salvation cannot be bought. It cannot be earned. It certainly is not deserved. It is the eternal Christmas present, wrapped in love, given with no expectations, no hidden agendas, no strings attached.

The late Bob Benson in *The Journey Home* shared a wonderful illustration about God's bountiful resources. He recalls the "olden days" when they had old-fashioned Sunday School picnics. They said, "We'll all meet at Sycamore Lodge in Shelby Park at 4:30 on Saturday. You bring your supper, and we'll furnish the iced tea."

"But if you were like me, you came home at the last minute. When you got ready to pack your picnic, all you could find in the refrigerator was one dried up piece of bologna and just enough mustard in the bottom of the jar so that you got it all over your knuckles trying to get into it. And just two slices of stale bread to go with it. So you made your bologna sandwich and wrapped it in an old brown bag and went to the picnic.

"When it came time to eat, you sat at the end of a table

and spread out your sandwich. But the folks who sat next to you brought a feast . . . fried chicken and baked beans and potato salad and homemade rolls and sliced tomatoes and pickles and olives and celery. And two big homemade chocolate pies to top it off.

"But they said to you, 'Why don't we just put it all together?'

"'No, I couldn't do that. I couldn't even think of it,' you murmured in embarrassment, with one eye on the chicken.

"'Oh, come on, there's plenty of chicken and plenty of pie and plenty of everything. And we just love bologna sandwiches. Let's just put it all together.'

And so you did and there you sat, eating like a king when you came like a pauper."*

> **We are debtors to give the gospel to every person in the same manner in which we have received it.**
> **—Phineas F. Bresee**

God offers every man, woman, and child a bountiful feast at His banquet table, rich food fit for a king and queen, prepared with loving affection—and all we have to bring is whatever we have, no matter how small, no matter how pitiful. Is there any better news than that?

For some reason, however, this *good news* (gospel) seems to be a difficult thing for many of us to share. Yet if we heard that the local supermarket was giving away T-bone steaks, "as many as your truck could carry," wouldn't we get on the phone and call our friends? If the car dealership down the street were offering brand-new BMWs for

*Bob Benson with Karen Dean Fry, *The Journey Home* (Kansas City: Beacon Hill Press of Kansas City, 1997), 108-9.

$100, wouldn't we shout it from the mountaintop? Then why are so many folks so reluctant to tell their coworkers, their neighbors, their family, and their friends about "the deal of a lifetime"? Is it guilt? Is it fear that we'll have to reveal our own sin? Is it worry that our friends will think we're trying to be better than they are? God offers *whosoever* a lifetime of peace and true happiness—and His offer lasts forever, time with no end.

Salvation is like receiving a gift. Paul says in Romans 6:23, "The wages of sin is death, but *the gift of God is eternal life in Christ Jesus our Lord*" (emphasis added). Salvation is like opening a door. John quotes the Master in Rev. 3:20—"Hear I am! I stand at the door and knock. If anyone hears my voice and *opens the door, I will come in and eat with him, and he with me*" (emphasis added). Salvation is like going through a door. John quotes Jesus in his Gospel as saying, "I am the gate; *whosoever enters through me will be saved.* He will come in and go out, and find pasture. The thief comes only to steal and kill and destroy; I have come that they might have life, and have it to the full" (John 10:9-10, emphasis added). Finally, salvation is like coming home. Jesus likens it in Luke 15 to the return of a wayward son. "We had to celebrate and be glad," the father says to his older son, "because this brother of yours was dead *and is alive again;* he was lost *and is found*" (Luke 15:32, emphasis added).

Until you tell him or her, a sinner might think he or she can gain salvation through some kind of human inheritance. This line of reasoning tells this person that along with brown eyes and black hair, he or she also inherited from his or her Christian mother and father eternal life. Another misconception among sinners is that salvation can be earned through some sort of human effort. That is to say that if enough good works are done, if enough benevolence is shown, then he or she can buy a ticket through the pearly gates. A third myth is that salvation can be had through the desires of others—if Mom and Dad pray hard enough, God will have to answer their prayers no matter how little the sinner might do in humble obedience to God.

THE ABCs OF EVANGELISM

Personal evangelism is always a one-on-one relationship, effective only as we build bridges of kinship with the person we are leading to the throne. Jesus showed us this time and time again during His life, and we would be foolish to stray from His model. The message might be delivered en masse, but it is received only through person-to-person contact in a moment of sincere prayer.

It is challenging to talk about evangelism. I feel a little like Dwight L. Moody when a young man come to him and said, "Mr. Moody, I don't like your witnessing plan."

Mr. Moody was a little surprised but asked, "Well, then, what plan do *you* use?"

"I really haven't found a plan I like," the young man replied.

"Then," said Moody, "I like my plan better than your plan."

Over the years I have developed a four-step process I call *The ABCs of a Personal Relationship with Christ*. Its simplicity reflects the method shown to us by Jesus under the New Covenant. No longer are we entangled with the Law, full of procedures and regulations and rules and punishments. Instead we are free! In personal evangelism, of course, the first step is always to pray beforehand that God will anoint you as you present the gospel to your friend or family member. The second step is to present the plan of salvation. The ABC method is patterned after the way I was led to the Lord when I was only four years old. "Boys and girls, receiving Jesus is as simple as ABC," my Sunday School teacher said. "First, Admit that you have sinned. It says in Rom. 3:23 that 'all have sinned and fall short of the glory of God.' Next, **B**elieve that Jesus Christ died for you. It says in John 1:12 that 'to all who received him, to those who believed in his name, he gave the right to become children of God.' And finally, **C**onfess that Jesus Christ is Lord of your life. It says in Romans 10:9-10 that 'if you confess with your mouth, "Jesus is Lord," and believe in your heart that God raised him from the dead, you will be saved.'"

After presenting the ABCs of salvation, you might use what I have dubbed the "how to go to heaven" pen. (I always carry a pen that contains the ABC plan of salvation.) Once you have explained that salvation is a gift, something freely given, ask the individual, "Would you believe me if I told you that I want to give you this pen?"

The answer is almost always, "Yes, I would believe you."

"But you don't have the pen right now, do you?" you might ask. "What do you need to do to get the pen?"

"Well," the person will say. "I'd need to reach out and take it from your hand."

"That's right," you say as you hand the person the pen. "And now it's yours. Free of charge. No questions asked. And so it is with receiving Christ as your Savior. All you have to do is reach out and take Him into your heart by faith."

The third step is to lead the person in "the sinner's prayer." It goes something like this: "Dear Lord Jesus, I know I'm a sinner. I believe that You died for my sins and rose from the grave. I now turn from my sins and invite You to come into my heart and life. I receive You as my personal Savior and follow You as my Lord. Amen." I have led hundreds of individuals in this prayer, and I have yet to remain unmoved as I see the face of the newborn Christian. Radiant. Excited. Grateful. Reborn! Every time I am amazed that so many Christians are so shy about sharing the gospel with others.

The last step is to give the new convert assurance that what has just happened to him or her is real and true. First John 5:11-12 says, "And this is the testimony: God has given us eternal life, and this life is in his Son. He who has the Son has life; he who does not have the Son of God does not have life."

I recommend developing an ABC networking plan. The idea came to me almost by accident, even though I believe God helped me see it. I was on a plane headed for San Francisco for a speaking engagement when the man seated next to me told me he worked for Amway, and I told him I was a pastor who worked with pastors. "My church sure needs a boost," he said, and before I knew what I was doing, I was telling him about the ABCs, handing him a pen, and discovering that he had a sincere relationship with the Lord. Through God's leading I began to draw circles on a napkin.

THE ABC NETWORKING PLAN

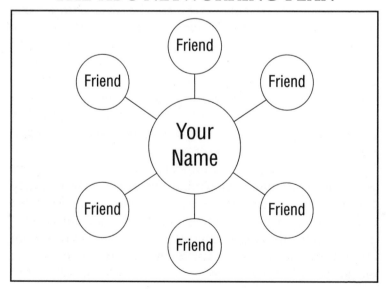

"Have you ever seen anything like this?" I asked him.

"It looks like what we do at Amway," he said.

"No," I said, "it's not Amway. It's Moses and the circles. If you were to ask Joe Victor [the chairman of the board at Amway at the time], he would tell you that they designed Amway around Moses' and Jethro's conversation when Moses was having problems with his melancholy spirit and organizational problems. Jethro told him, 'This is the way you do it. You build circles.'"

The networking plan consists of seven circles—one in the middle containing your name and six around the middle containing the names of friends, acquaintances, co-workers, and family members you wish to lead to the Lord. After you have filled in all seven circles, begin to pray every day for each name on the network, including your own. Then start to share activities with them, taking them to ball games, having them over for a night of games and refreshment, bringing them to picnics and parties. On the surface this may sound manipulative—making friends with them just to bash them over the head with a Bible when they least expect it. That's not what happens. Eventually, when *you* least expect it, the door will open for you to share why you seem to be different, happy, content, at peace. You'll be surprised how natural it seems to present the plan of salvation. Another thing you might try is to invite them to an event that is purposefully designed to reach the unsaved and unchurched—a revival meeting, a religious concert, a gospel presentation.

When my son Seth and his cousin Trent were five years old, they played on a soccer team in Oklahoma City. My wife, my brother, his wife, and I went to every game and began to talk to the other parents at the games, often going out for ice cream afterward. We never said a word about being pastors—we just fellowshipped. After several weeks passed, they asked what we did for a living, but when we told them we were pastors, it was no big deal. We yelled at the referees just like they did and shared a lot of good times together. Gradually an interesting thing began to happen. I would look out over the congregation on Sunday morning and notice that many of those families were there. Eventually most of the team members started attending—some have even served on the church board!

EVENT EVANGELISM

As a pastor, it is your responsibility to provide opportunities for your people to invite their unsaved, unchurched friends. While pastoring in Nashville, we discovered that about 92 percent of visitors come to church because of a friend or family member. The first step, of course, is to encourage your members to invite their friends to these special events. Be sure to remind them that you will be sharing the ABC plan there—it's best not to surprise anyone. Let the Holy Spirit do the surprising and convicting. The second step is to advertise the event according to your desired target group, be it baby boomers, baby busters, senior citizens, or whoever. The third step is to use a variety of creative and innovative events to reach as many segments of your community as you can: dinner dramas, concerts, musicals, seminars, revivals, films, workshops, crafts, ball games, and so on. The fourth step is to design a response form for each special event. For example, you might plan to share the ABC plan at the midpoint of the event. Be sure to ask *everyone* to fill out the information form and ask *everyone* to pray the sinner's prayer aloud. This will help guests to feel comfortable in participating. This sample form can be used to elicit information from visiting friends.

The final step may be the most important: follow up the event with a phone call, a letter, a personal visit within 24 hours of the event. This immediate demonstration of interest and shepherding will be appreciated sincerely.

HARVEST CELEBRATION

Name _____

Address _____

City _____ State _____ Zip _____

Phone _____

___ TONIGHT, I prayed the ABC prayer to invite Jesus Christ to become my personal Savior and Lord.

___ Please send me additional help on the Christian life.

___ I am active in another church.

___ I am member/regular attender of First Church.

___ I would be interested in receiving information on future First Church events.

I heard about HARVEST CHRISTMAS from:

___ Radio Advertisement   ___ Television

___ Newspaper   ___ Posters

___ Personal Invitation   ___ Friend/Family

___ Metro Bus   ___ Church Announcement

___ Other (please specify)

OUTREACH TODAY

The gospel never changes. Jesus Christ is the same yesterday, today, forever. Outreach methods *do* change, though. Those that worked in the '70s and '80s do not work anymore, and it is futile (and perhaps a bit vain) to insist on using outdated means to convey the good news of salvation. In their book *The Issachar Factor*, Gary McIntosh and Glen Martin have outlined what worked *then* and what works *now:*

That was then . . .	This is now . . .
Door-to-door	Friend-to-friend
Confrontational	Relational
Tracts	Multimedia
Hard sell	Soft sell
Evangelism committees	Evangelism teams
Guilt-driven	Love-motivated
Evangelism as a duty	Outreach as a lifestyle

I'll never forget a soul-winning conference I attended many years ago. The trainer of personal witnessing said, "I went soul-winnin' and found this ol' boy out there in the backyard. He's sittin' there with a six-pack of beer, sportin' this tank top and Bermuda shorts, barefoot and draggin' on a big ol' cigar. I go up to him and try to tell him about the Lord, but he isn't payin' one bit of attention to me, so I just grab his matches. I strike one of those matches and stick it up against his bare foot and say, 'Son, if you think this is hot, hell is hotter!' That ol' boy immediately fell down on his knees, and he commenced to prayin' to God and got right." Most of the time evangelism doesn't work like that anymore. It just might get you killed! We have to relate to people and build relationships in today's society before we can get anything accomplished for the Kingdom.

Target groups are often the stumblingblock to effective evangelism, because each group has different needs and desires. Senior adults are defined as anyone born before 1930. They grew up during the Great Depression, and many of them fought in World War II. Their thrift, patriotism, and hard work established them as the foundation of our culture today. You're not going to reach them through gimmicks and frivolity. Although they like a good time, they want substance. The builders were born between 1930 and 1945, and they grew up while America and the rest of the world was rebuilding. They know what it's like to start from scratch and watch something grow from nothing. The baby boomers were born between 1946 and 1964 and represent 77 million people, over a third of our population, but only about 25 million are in church today. According to George Gallup, "The baby boomers are a floating population, religiously speaking. They are consumers of religion, shopping around."

Elmer Towns suggests four reasons that baby boomers are unique:

1. They were the first generation to grow up with mass availability and acceptance of birth control. When they were born, only 18 percent of the female population worked outside the home. Fifty years later, that percentage has neared 90.

2. They were the first generation to grow up with the atomic bomb and the threat of total destruction. As a baby boomer, I can remember those civil defense drills at my little elementary school in Baileysville, West Virginia. That siren would start winding up, and 200 children jumped under their desks with their hands over their heads—as if that would protect us from nuclear holocaust! It is no wonder so many of us are intent on instant gratification and grabbing for all the gusto—we all thought we were going to die before we were old enough to die.

3. This was the generation that grew up under the tutelage of Dr. Benjamin Spock, whose book on child-rear-

ing sold 30 million copies, encouraging parents not to spank their children and not to make children feel guilty.

4. This generation grew up in prosperity with lots of money to be earned. That has done two things—made it the most educated generation in history and made it the most indebted generation in history. I am the first Toler in the history of my family in West Virginia to get a college education, and I am so thankful to my mother and stepfather for seeing to it that I got through college.

Baby boomers were also the first generation to grow up with television. No other medium has had quite the profound effect on the way we live as the screen in the middle of our living room. From news to entertainment, we have shrunk the world to fit into a 19" square box, and today's generation cannot even fathom a life that did not include *Seinfeld*, MTV, and *Monday Night Football*. I can remember when our family "went modern and liberal" and bought a little black-and-white television set when we moved to Ohio. You see, our previous church had always preached the evils of television, so we had to move from there before we could get one.

Quite a phenomenon is occurring all across America today—baby boomers are coming back to church. Doug Murren, pastor of Foursquare East Side Church in Vancouver, Washington, offers seven reasons for this occurrence in his book *Baby Boomerang*. First is depression. *Time* magazine reports that over 18 million people in American are depressed. The American Medical Association says that next to aspirin/nonaspirin pain reliever, the two most popular drugs on the market today are Valium and Prozac. Most of the victims of depression are baby boomers. The second reason baby boomers are coming back to church, according to Murren, is "New Age burnout." This generation has tried crystal balls, channeling, and calling 1-900-HOROSCOPE and have concluded that those things don't work. The third reason is "Black Monday." Along with failing banks and a collapse in America's oil industry in the 1980s came the day the stock market plunged. All of a sudden the baby boomers began to realize that money was fleeting. Murren's fourth reason for the return to church by baby boomers is family values. These people are coming back to church because they have children at home whom they want to raise with a strong ethical foundation. Sixty percent of boomer households still have children at home.

The fifth reason is social activism. We have talked about the social conscience of the Church, but most of these baby boomers have a latent desire to change society. They were marchers and protesters. The sixth reason is companionship. Many of this generation are single again, and church is an important place to meet their needs. Some of them are even looking for a "good mate." The seventh reason is sheer boredom. Television no longer cuts it; the *New York Times* crossword puzzle is too hard. They are coming back to find deeper fulfillment in life.

The children of the boomers are called the "baby busters," representing 39 million in our population. One of the primary distinctives of this generation is the chasm between them and their predecessors. Whereas the generation gap between the boomers and builders was because of a new morality called "free love," this new gap is centered in economics. The busters blame the boomers for getting this country into a debt that will end only when America declares bankruptcy. Another characteristic unique to the busters is that they are the most incarcerated generation in history. Busters have single-handedly caused a movement in prison reform. A third trait of this generation is that they are the first in the 20th century that are less well off financially than their parents were at the same age. Instead of anchoring themselves in careers, they seem to be content to hold down "Mcjobs." Many of them are coming back home to live with their parents, often taking more than four years to finish their college education.

A very positive outcome of this is that they are committed to family. They are sick and tired of the messes their boomer parents have made with marriages and the breakup of the home. Some sociologists claim that the upward trend in divorce statistics will begin reversing itself by 2000, because the baby busters are making a serious commitment to marriage, evidenced in part by the increase in the average age of marriage—now nearly 25.

Finally, this new generation is the most conservative group since the 1920s. They are listening to conservative talk—on the radio, on the television, in the classroom, and at their churches. What they are saying is that if the current political structure does not get it right soon, they will form a party to get it right.

How do we reach these people? The first step is to replace traditional programming with more informality. The new generations are not into form, formula, and format. They don't like straight rows and lectures—they want to see each others' faces and discuss things.

A second change is to stress relationships rather than structures. Look at the decrease in memberships across the country in civic clubs. Boomers and busters don't like the structure of these organizations.

Third, you must meet these younger people in their arena of thought. They want to talk about issues of the day, so you must schedule series of talks or sermons on hot topics. Should a Christian be involved in politics? What is our mission in the marketplace? Where should we stand on abortion? Gun control? Capital punishment? Divorce and remarriage?

Fourth, you must simplify your message. Bob Kreitner has written a former top-10 book on management, and he says, "Corporations need to simplify so an eight-year-old can understand the flow of the corporation." Jesus said that unless we come to Him as little children, we will not find Him. Well, how can we approach Him that way unless He speaks through you that way? Someone wrote to Billy Graham not long ago and said, "Dr. Graham, send us a preacher. P.S. We want a preacher who does not know Greek and who has not been to the Holy Land." Talk about a tragic indictment against the clergy! I'll tell you this: if we sound like a travelogue, if we speak in the Greek or spew in the Hebrew, then we're missing the point of the gospel. The news is simple—let's make it equally easy to understand instead of showing off our education and experiences.

Fifth, emphasize the integrity of the Christian lifestyle. People watch more than they listen, so if you're not practicing what you preach or walking what you talk, then it won't matter how polished your speech might be. It will fall on deaf ears.

Sixth, share the ministry with them. If you want to see the effects of good leadership or bad leadership, you ought to visit a volunteer staff sometime. Whether it's a civic group, church group, or college group, its growth will depend on the amount of workload that is shared. In groups where the leader insists on doing it "my way," he or she will usually end up doing all the work. But when the leader delegates work fairly and democratically, everyone feels important and contributes. People like to be a part of that kind of dynamic.

Finally, become evangelistically sensitive. Instead of pounding on the pulpit and screaming, "You're all going to end up in a lake of fire and burn forever in hell!" you might simply look them in the eye and say gently, "It is true—we've all sinned and come short of the glory of God. But the gift of God is eternal life through Jesus Christ our Lord. To receive that gift, all we have to do is invite Him into our hearts."

Why is it that so many people don't go to church anymore? According to Bill Hybels, pastor of the Willow Creek Community Church, they claim that the church is always asking them for money, they don't like the music, they can't relate to the message, the services don't meet their needs, and the pastor makes them feel guilty.

Margie Morris addresses the baby boomer and buster generations in her book, *Tools for Building Your Volunteer Ministry.* She says that to attract the younger generation, you must do the following:

TOOLS FOR BUILDING A VOLUNTEER MINISTRY
1. Provide an excellent nursery.
2. Build faith-to-life connections.
3. Address contemporary issues.
4. Mix fellowship and volunteer work.
5. Recruit for short-term assignments.
6. Encourage team teaching and group fellowship.
7. Cater fellowship dinners.
8. Provide Bible study.
9. Develop an outstanding Christian education program.
10. Schedule worship services at times other than Sunday morning.
11. Start new programs on a regular basis.
12. Publicize well.

The fastest-growing segment of our population is the senior adults, at three times the rate of the national population. With improved health care and better lifestyles, life expectancy is on a continual rise. The number of people in the United States who have reached their 65th birthday is now larger than the entire population of Canada. Two-thirds of all the people who have ever lived to age 65 are alive today, according to American church growth statistics.

As this general population increases, the local church had better be prepared to meet its needs. Seniors have more time available for volunteer activities than any other segment of the church. In fact, they average two to three times as many available hours for church-related activities as any other age-group in the church. They also have the largest amount of discretionary funds. Even though baby boomers are the wealthiest, they are also the deepest in debt. In any given year, a senior adult member will give seven times the amount that a baby boomer will give in the same church. As a baby boomer pastor once told his congregation, "If our seniors die, we boomers have had it! We won't be able to pay the bills." Senior adults also tend to be less transient—they move almost half as often as the national population average.

One way to reach this generation is to plan friendship-building events. At one of the churches I have pastored, the seniors loved to board the church bus every month and go somewhere together: the mountains; a resort restaurant; a nearby town for catfish, hush puppies, grits, and cornbread. Relationships don't become less important as we grow older—they become more important.

> **While the whole world has been multiplying, we have been making additions to the church.**
> **—D. James Kennedy**

MARKETING THE CHURCH

To market the local church, we have to be on the cutting edge. Here are four ideas to help:

PRODUCT. In the church the product is relationships. The world talks about having a product—our government calls it the "gross national product." In the church each person reproduces after his or her own kind, so what we have to market is relationships: "You can find a friend in this fellowship. Why, you can even find companionship!"

PRICE. That is the world's answer. *Our* price, however, is commitment: "When you join our church, you are going to have to get involved. It is going to take time and effort from you. We are not going to give you parking passes and privileges. In fact, we may even ask you to park in the parking lot next door."

PLACE. What does a Realtor say are the three most important words in business? Location. Location. Location. For the church, the word "place" means "presence of believers." I have often noted this slogan for my local churches. "There is no church like this church anywhere near this church. This is the church!" Acts 4:31 says, "When they had prayed, the place was shaken where they were assembled" (KJV).

PROMOTION. What are you doing to increase the flow of guests into your church? How are you getting people to come to church? How do you treat visitors when they enter your sanctuary? Do you introduce yourself, hand them a songbook, and invite them to be a part of the family of God? What do you do after they have come and gone? Do you follow up or merely hope they come back on their own? I think having guests for dinner is similar to having visitors in church. I know that when we have someone over to dinner, my wife and I knock ourselves out getting the house clean, the food prepared, the table set, and the atmosphere just right. We want our company to feel both at home and like royalty. They are special people. That's the way the church needs to treat its "company," but they need to know it takes effort, preparation, and special attention. Hospitality doesn't just happen.

Today there are so many ways a pastor and church leaders can market their local church. First, the property should be kept clean, painted, and well-marked. This includes good lighting at night with appropriate signage that is perpendicular to the street. Another easy way to keep the church name out there is by using a two- or three-line message in the yellow pages. If funding is available, a 30-second or 60-second spot on the radio during drive time is an excellent way to publicize your church. Same for television time. For special events at the holidays, use press releases and advertisements in your local newspapers. For programs and campaigns, develop attractive pamphlets and brochures to distribute in the community or by mail.

One Oklahoma church I know offers night classes for the community. They call it "Rooms for Improvement" and mail out 15,000 flyers. Last time they had 483 people respond to topics such as "A Snippet of Single Life," "Basic Computer Literacy," "Discovering Your Type," "Healing Aspects of Anger," "Building Your Marriage," "Strengthening Family Ties," "Making the Bible User-Friendly," "Life Choices," "The Power of a Man's Word," "There's Something You Need to Know About Your Child," "Stress," and "Self-Esteem." Volunteers from the congregation who have special training in these areas teach the classes. The church pays for any materials needed (within reason), and publicity is predominantly word-of-mouth with pamphlets and newspaper supplements.

I have always had what I call the "Fat Club," because I have to fight the battle of the bulge all the time (currently I'm winning, but it hasn't always been that way). When I served as pastor in Nashville, I asked a Weight Watchers instructor to conduct Weight Watchers sessions at the church on Wednesday evenings. Following the session we also offered a low-fat dinner with a salad bar at a minimal cost of $2.00 for participants. Pretty soon we had a significant group of people in the Weight Watchers meetings. And it wasn't long before we noticed them staying for Wednesday night Bible study. Seminars, musicals, dramas, and so on can also serve as event evangelism opportunities for the local church.

C H A P T E R   5

FOLLOW-UP DISCIPLESHIP
VS.
"Y'ALL COME BACK!"

*Twenty-five percent of all first-time visitors are
likely to join your church. Seventy-five percent of
all return visitors are likely to join your church.*
—Jim Stocks

THE ASSIMILATION PRINCIPLE

Assimilation begins by opening the front door and concludes by closing the back door. That may seem oversimplified, but there's more truth behind it than you might think.

Across a Crowded Room

I must confess I loved her. We tried to see each other at least once a week—more often if we could. We would catch each other's eye across a crowded room, exchange a wink and a knowing smile, and then thread our way through that crowd until at last we embraced and kissed. She would tell me how she loved me, and I would swear my affection to her. You see, we had fallen in love the first time we met, and though many relationships ebb and flow over the years, ours never did; the love and deep feelings waxed stronger with time.

Many times her husband would catch us, but he never seemed to mind. He was just as likely to be hugging my wife—or my kids—or waiting to hug me and say, "God bless you and your family." I was in love with his wife, it's true, but I loved him in just the same way.

And I probably always will love Reuel and Irma Douglas, the first couple to greet us and make us feel welcome at this church some 16 years ago. We were in our 20s; they were in their 60s, but there was no generation gap. They've both crossed over to the other shore recently, but their spirit and memory linger near my heart. I can see the twinkle in their eyes, hear their gracious and loving works, and feel the warmth they exuded. It's a shame they're not here to seek out and welcome visitors as they did with us. Guess I'll need to pick up where they left off, engaging new folks in conversation, trying to make them feel at home. I'll be looking across a crowded sanctuary to catch the eye of someone new, but all the while it will be Irma and Reuel I'll be remembering.

—Jim Priest
Lay Leader, Oklahoma City First Church of the Nazarene
(Used with permission)

The process of evangelizing is not complete until those who have responded to the claims of Christ are active, functioning members of the local church. In other words, the goal in evangelism is not just to get a decision—it is to make disciples, according to Robert Bast.

In his book *Attracting New Members,* Bast identifies three stages in assimilating new people into the fellowship of the local church level: testing, affiliation, and assimilation. In the first stage, you must identify the prospects who have the potential to be assimilated into the church. There are many methods of doing this. One old-fashioned way is to have a clipboard stationed on every pew in the church with sheets of paper on which everyone on the row is to put his or her name, address, phone number, and whether or not he or she is a regular attender or a visitor. When I used this method in my churches, we would ask the last person on the row to look over all the names on his or her row and then pass the clipboard back to where it originated so that everyone else on the row could also read all the names as it was passed back.

A more common method used today is the guest card. It provides the same information but in a more anonymous way, and you know as well as I that the thing a first-time visitor wants more than anything else is anonymity. On it you should include a section that asks for information in particular interests: salvation, consultation with the pastor, membership, baptism, Sunday School, children's ministries, and so on. Another section could focus on how he or she heard about your church so that you might be able to detect ways you can market your church more effectively.

Once you have established a list of names, it is always wise to provide some sort of survey for your guests to let you know what they think of your congregation and services. In one church I pastored, the people believed that they were a very friendly church; in fact, they prided themselves in their friendliness. Yet week after week I heard visitors say they got the cold shoulder when they entered the building. That is a most lethal combination when you are trying to grow a church.

FRIENDSHIP REGISTRATION FOR EVERYONE PRESENT
Please register and help us to be a friendly church.

(1) Record your name and check or enter other pertinent information.
(2) Pass the pad to the next person.
(3) When it reaches the end of the row pass it back, noting the names of others.
(4) After the benediction, greet your fellow worshipers by name.

MEMBERS/REGULAR ATTENDERS
Name _____
New Address _____
New Phone _____ New Zip _____
☐ Member ☐ Regular Attender

MEMBERS/REGULAR ATTENDERS
Name _____
New Address _____
New Phone _____ New Zip _____
☐ Member ☐ Regular Attender

MEMBERS/REGULAR ATTENDERS
Name _____
New Address _____
New Phone _____ New Zip _____
☐ Member ☐ Regular Attender

MEMBERS/REGULAR ATTENDERS
Name _____
New Address _____
New Phone _____ New Zip _____
☐ Member ☐ Regular Attender

MEMBERS/REGULAR ATTENDERS
Name _____
New Address _____
New Phone _____ New Zip _____
☐ Member ☐ Regular Attender

MEMBERS/REGULAR ATTENDERS
Name _____
New Address _____
New Phone _____ New Zip _____
☐ Member ☐ Regular Attender

MEMBERS/REGULAR ATTENDERS
Name _____
New Address _____
New Phone _____ New Zip _____
☐ Member ☐ Regular Attender

MEMBERS/REGULAR ATTENDERS
Name _____
New Address _____
New Phone _____ New Zip _____
☐ Member ☐ Regular Attender

VISITORS
Name _____ Phone _____
Address _____
City _____ Zip _____
Age of Children _____
Church Member? _____
☐ FIRST-TIME VISITOR ☐ SINGLE
☐ MARRIED ☐ YOUTH

VISITORS
Name _____ Phone _____
Address _____
City _____ Zip _____
Age of Children _____
Church Member? _____
☐ FIRST-TIME VISITOR ☐ SINGLE
☐ MARRIED ☐ YOUTH

VISITORS
Name _____ Phone _____
Address _____
City _____ Zip _____
Age of Children _____
Church Member? _____
☐ FIRST-TIME VISITOR ☐ SINGLE
☐ MARRIED ☐ YOUTH

VISITORS
Name _____ Phone _____
Address _____
City _____ Zip _____
Age of Children _____
Church Member? _____
☐ FIRST-TIME VISITOR ☐ SINGLE
☐ MARRIED ☐ YOUTH

VISITORS
Name _____ Phone _____
Address _____
City _____ Zip _____
Age of Children _____
Church Member? _____
☐ FIRST-TIME VISITOR ☐ SINGLE
☐ MARRIED ☐ YOUTH

Turn to the next sheet when this one is full. Last person in row, please return pad to starting point.

Date _____		
Mr./Mrs./Miss _____		
Address _____ Phone _____		
City _____ State _____ Zip _____		

☐ FIRST-TIME GUEST
I heard about First Church through
  ☐ A Friend
  ☐ Radio
  ☐ Newspaper
  ☐ Other _____
☐ Member
☐ Regular Attender
☐ Return Guest
	I AM INTERESTED IN:
	☐ Accepting Christ as my Savior
	☐ Consultation with the pastoral staff
	☐ Membership in this church
	☐ Baptism
	☐ A Sunday School class
	☐ Helping in this church's ministries
	☐ Being discipled
	☐ Children's ministries
	☐ Teen's ministries
	☐ Adult ministries
	☐ Being placed on mailing list
	☐ Pastor's Welcome Class
		AGE
		☐ Under 12 yrs.
		☐ 7th-8th grade
		☐ 9th-12th grade
		☐ 18-22
		☐ 23-34
		☐ 35-50
		☐ 51-64
		☐ 65 and over
		
		Marital Status
		☐ Single
		☐ Married

Do You Have a Church Home? ☐ Yes ☐ No		

The survey should contain questions concerning how and where the guest was greeted, the friendliness and hospitality of the Sunday School class, the warmth of those sitting near the guest in the worship service, the ease of access to the facility, the guest's feelings during the visit, the perception of the guest's children, any negatives, and the probability of his or her return. A sample survey I have used with success in several churches is as follows:

GUEST SURVEY

Your assistance in completing this survey would be a great help to us as we examine ourselves and commit to making improvement.

1. We were greeted
   in the parking lot? ☐ Yes ☐ No
   at the entrance to the building? ☐ Yes ☐ No
   at the entrance to the sanctuary? ☐ Yes ☐ No

2. If you attended a Sunday School class
   Did you feel welcomed in the class? ☐ Yes ☐ No
   Did you meet the teacher? ☐ Yes ☐ No
   Did those sitting near you introduce themselves? ☐ Yes ☐ No
   Did anyone offer to take you to the sanctuary? ☐ Yes ☐ No
   Did anyone ask you to sit with them during the service? ☐ Yes ☐ No
   Did you receive a lunch invitation from anyone? ☐ Yes ☐ No

3. Did those sitting near you in the sanctuary
   greet you before the service? ☐ Yes ☐ No
   greet you during the fellowship time? ☐ Yes ☐ No
   greet you after the service? ☐ Yes ☐ No

4. Where you able to easily locate
   Visitor Parking ☐ Yes ☐ No ☐ N/A
   Nursery ☐ Yes ☐ No ☐ N/A
   Rest Room Facilities ☐ Yes ☐ No ☐ N/A
   Information Central ☐ Yes ☐ No ☐ N/A
   Visitor's Booth ☐ Yes ☐ No ☐ N/A
   Sanctuary ☐ Yes ☐ No ☐ N/A

5. Since your visit have you received
   a call or letter from a staff member? ☐ Yes ☐ No
   a call or letter from someone in the Sunday School class? ☐ Yes ☐ No
   an invitation for fellowship? ☐ Yes ☐ No
   an invitation to return? ☐ Yes ☐ No

6. During my visit at First Church I felt
   ☐ Love ☐ Apathy
   ☐ Warmth ☐ Coldness
   ☐ Important ☐ Unimportant
   ☐ Happiness ☐ Sadness
   ☐ Accepted ☐ Lonely
   ☐ Enthusiasm ☐ Indifference
   ☐ Interest ☐ Disinterest
   ☐ Peace ☐ Unrest

7. Did someone help you find your Sunday School class? ☐ Yes ☐ No

8. If you attended accompanied by children, please answer the following
   questions?
   Did you feel comfortable leaving your children in the nursery or in their
   Sunday School class? ☐ Yes ☐ No
   Was a name tag placed on your child? ☐ Yes ☐ No
   Was the teacher notified as to where to find parents
   if needed? ☐ Yes ☐ No

9. Did you experience anything negative that we should be
   aware of? ☐ Yes ☐ No

   If yes, please feel free to comment: _____

10. Overall, I would describe First Church as:
    ☐ Extremely Friendly
    ☐ Very Friendly
    ☐ Friendly
    ☐ Unfriendly
    ☐ Cold

11. We plan to return?
    ☐ Yes ☐ No

Although it may not be obvious, one place to be certain that guests feel welcome is in the bathrooms. Face it—a home might be a showcase house fit for a magazine cover, but if there is soap scum on the bathroom sink and unflushed material in the toilet, the lasting impression will inevitably be negative. Same with restaurants—the food might be great, the service superb, but if the bathroom looks and smells like a high school locker room, I won't be back! Not only should everything be clean, but soap, toilet paper, and paper towels should be well stocked. It might be a good idea to have one of your ushers check the bathrooms periodically during worship time to make sure things aren't out of hand. This same attention should be paid to drinking fountains, kitchens, and coffeepots too.

Another area in which your church is tested weekly by guests is in the welcoming department. If your church is mid-sized or large, you would be wise to station some of your greeters in the parking lot, especially if the lot is large or some distance from the sanctuary. I know many large churches that use golf carts or vans to provide shuttles to and from the lot, particularly during inclement weather. There ought to be ample space allotted to guest-only parking near the facility and someone in the lot to be sure the handicapped parking spaces remain available to those who truly need them. I know of one church where parking greeters write a personal welcome on note cards and place them on the driver's side of the windshield. It leaves a lasting good impression on visitors to know that someone took the time to notice that they were there and thank them for coming.

Once guests are inside the church, they should be met by a friendly, outgoing person who makes sure they get the proper church materials and are personally ushered to the appropriate Sunday School class or sanctuary pew. Nothing could be more distasteful and disconcerting than to walk into a strange place and be left completely alone to wander the hallways.

Provide training for greeters and ushers, including a tip sheet on dos and don'ts. For instance, *"Do* offer a hand or arm if footing seems uncertain, but *don't* insist on hugging someone or putting your arm around him or her." Or *"Do* feel free to make small talk as you walk with the individual, but *don't* drill the individual for personal information." Once the greeters and ushers have been trained in the classroom, publicly commission them in an appropriate setting, either during a service, dinner, or in the newsletter. At a later time celebrate their commitment in a social setting, where you can also evaluate and schedule future events. Win Arn once said, "When people walk into a church for the first time, the greeter or usher who welcomes them is, to them, the church. The opinions they are forming of the particular usher who is helping them are the opinions they are forming of the church."

Growing churches are learning that a welcome center is a valuable tool in their hospitality and, therefore, retention efforts. This center needs to be staffed by friendly members of your church who will greet all guests and return visitors, distribute helpful information, escort them to appropriate areas, and most important, secure their names, addresses, and phone numbers. Someone needs to be at the center throughout the Sunday School hour for guests who arrive too late for class but too early for worship. Couches, easy chairs, coffee, and other refreshments should be nearby so each guest feels at home. One danger I have found in making this area so inviting, however, is that many members loiter there and make visitors feel uncomfortably outnumbered.

All these amenities are important to your efforts in providing guests with all they need to feel welcomed, but your primary concern is to be a church where they can *experience* God in worship. Herb Miller said, "If the worship service fails to meet the needs of first-time visitors, no amount of friendliness can convert them to joiners."

Robert Bast defines the second stage of assimilation as the affiliation stage. This includes faithful and prompt follow-up, which is a crucial component for winning potential members. When contact is made within 24 hours of the initial visit, 85 percent of church guests return the following week. When follow-up contact is made within 72 hours, 60 percent come back. But if contact is delayed a week or more, only about 15 percent will return to try your church again. And we have found that laypersons see a much higher percentage of return of visitors when they make the contact than when the pastor makes the call—nearly twice as high. That may be for several reasons, but guests certainly tend to identify more with people just like them than they do with the pastor. And let's not discount the fact that the pastor is a paid emissary, whereas the layperson is a volunteer. That speaks volumes to the guest.

There are six steps a church might consider in developing an effective follow-up program. The first is prayer. Nothing else matters if God is not centrally placed in the process, so I have always appointed a group of people I call my Abrahams, who commit to personal and corporate prayer as we endeavor to grow God's kingdom. These are usually people who are strongly behind the evangelistic ministry of the church but do not feel gifted in face-to-face outreach. I have found sometimes that shut-ins and other elderly are magnificent prayer warriors who know just where to find the throne of grace.

A second step is to make a phone call to each guest within 24 hours of his or her visit. Again, this ministry is often best suited to those who are a bit reserved but like to converse. These Barnabas people deliver the message: "Welcome. Hope to see you next Sunday. Let's meet at the west door."

Third, the pastor writes a personal note to each guest. Some may choose to type these, but a handwritten letter adds a genuinely personal touch. Unfortunately, my handwriting is more suitable for writing a prescription than it is for welcoming folks to church, but I take extra care with these notes. I use a small note card with the church logo or other identifying inscription printed on the front for immediate recognition.

A fourth strategy is to develop a gift-evangelism team. Some years ago I started using the Bakers of Men program. A group of men baked loaves of bread each week to be distributed to guests on the Sunday of their visit. It is not necessary, of course, to limit yourself to loaves of bread; pies, cookies, or cakes are equally effective in making people feel welcomed. One church gives out jars of Smuckers jam, on the back of which they attach a note that says, "Your visit has left us a sweet taste."

The fifth step is perhaps the most involved and certainly the most work—it is the pastor's brunch. Over the years I have tried many methods with regard to assimilation, but without a doubt this has been the most productive. Wes Williams, a staff member in Nashville, gave me the idea. I had tried having guests in my home; I had tried giving staff members allowances to take guests out to dinner; I had even worked hard to get people in the congregation to invite guests home with them after services. But these days most people have too much to do to go home to eat after church. In fact, my brother, who is a pastor also, has been to a parishioner's home after Sunday morning church only once in his 10 years at that location. Nothing seemed to work until this idea came along.

We decided to hold a brunch one Sunday noon every five weeks, inviting every person who had visited our church over that five-week period along with the church staff, who, by the way, do not really sit at a table much because they are circulating around the room during the meal, getting acquainted with the people. We soon realized how much preparation was involved to make these brunches successful and formed a Pastor's Brunch Ministry Action Team, made up of key individuals who had the gift of hospitality. They were in charge of registration, name tags, greeting folks at the door, and being table hosts. We found round tables were best, but any table that allows face-to-face contact would work. Instead of a self-serve banquet table, it is much more comfortable for your guests to have servers who will bring the meals to the table. Alternating Sunday School classes to host is an easy way to get the whole church involved in this.

The Brunch Team is also responsible for decorations, because the room needs to have a warm, inviting atmosphere with lots of color. We use balloon bouquets at each table rather than floral bouquets because they're more informal, and the visiting children can then take them home afterward. No matter where you plan to have your pastor's brunch, be sure the room is big enough and well-suited for company.

Send out formal invitations for the brunch, just as you might send out invitations for a party at your house. Include the menu, the location and directions to that location, and the approximate time the event will be over. Instead of asking for a response (RSVP), call each guest to see if he or she will be able to come. This way your cooks or caterers will be able to plan more accurately, remembering that it's always better to have too much than to have too little. Churches that have used this strategy most effectively include a different menu for the children. Whereas a grownup will enjoy croissants and fruit salad, a child prefers a hot dog and potato chips.

One final idea is to have the church photographer come by and take pictures of the people so members will be able to place a face with a name more readily. Post the pictures and names of guests who attended the pastor's brunch on the bulletin board in the foyer so that everyone in the church has easy access.

The main purpose of the brunch is to assimilate newcomers more effectively into the church family. I have discovered that if a person can make a friend in the church, he or she will stay in the church; and conversely, if a guest remains friendless, chances are he or she will be attending another church soon. Name tags and introductions around the table are very important. Another tool is the guest packet, which contains information about the church and includes a recent newsletter, a Bible bookmark, an *ABC How to Go to Heaven* pen, or other appropriate gifts and information. Consider having a staff member's child welcome the other children by offering each one a box of animal crackers or a pack of bubble gum. The written information and the opportunity to visit with each staff member personally will give the guest a better sense of where he or she might plug in to your programs and ministries.

Small churches can carry out this program, even if the brunch must be held in the pastor's home and the menu is Hamburger Helper. The joy of being able to spend time with your guests is what matters. Over the years we've found that 86 percent of the people invited to brunch came back to our church.

The sixth step is a welcome class that is designed to share the vision of the local church. It is a four-week class that covers vision, confidence-building, communication, and commitment. Sometime during this class give students a notebook that includes sections on Studies in the Word, Prayer Concerns, Journalizing with God, and Worship/ Sermon Notes.

After this class, enroll students in a four-week gift discovery class. In the first session, individuals complete a personality profile designed by Florence Littauer. This is important for future recruitment of various ministries in the church. In the second week they are asked about their passions, hobbies, vocational goals, and ministry goals. Consider an interest and skills survey to see if they like to sing, play an instrument, do plumbing, carpentry, painting, whatever. In the last two weeks, explore their spiritual gifts. Using the Unwrapping Your Spiritual Gifts profile is a good way of doing that. Each of these tools is important as you guide people into the ministries that will be the most fulfilling to them. Finding the ministry fit that blends the individual's unique interests, giftedness, and personality will maximize his or her satisfaction and effectiveness.

The third four-week class is a discipleship class, during which people are introduced to the church's belief system, declaration of faith, rationale behind the church's creeds, and so on. Supply a small booklet that will capsulize this information. In the second week, discuss core values: integrity, personal holiness, and so on. And ask if they can identify with them. The third week consider biblical stewardship. Baby boomers, busters, and now generation Xers must be trained how to give. Distribute a complimentary box of tithing envelopes with their names stamped on them. The last week of class is about lay ministry. Before these students become a part of your fellowship, ask that they make a commitment to the Body of Christ to be involved in ministry, both in and out of the church. When you formally introduce these new members to the church, you'll be able to say, "He will be a part of our prayer ministry," or "She will be helping us out in our college ministry."

This whole series of introductory classes fills a quarter (12 weeks), and by the time each person has completed it, he or she will be ready to become an active member in the work of building God's kingdom at your local church.

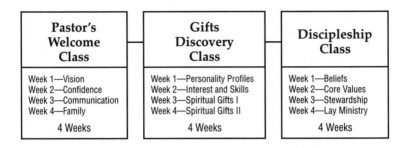

Pastor's Welcome Class	Gifts Discovery Class	Discipleship Class
Week 1—Vision Week 2—Confidence Week 3—Communication Week 4—Family	Week 1—Personality Profiles Week 2—Interest and Skills Week 3—Spiritual Gifts I Week 4—Spiritual Gifts II	Week 1—Beliefs Week 2—Core Values Week 3—Stewardship Week 4—Lay Ministry
4 Weeks	4 Weeks	4 Weeks

After 12 weeks of the previous classes, the time for commitment has arrived. This may be as simple as a commitment to a small group (Sunday School class, choir, ushering team, and so on), a commitment to a friendship (often forged at the pastor's brunch or through a Sunday School class), a commitment to Christ, a commitment to church membership, or a commitment to grow.

The assimilation ministry in a local church looks a lot like a baseball diamond. Imagine one right now: at home plate is the initial attraction to your church. It could be the music program being piped to the parking lot, the person at the front door who makes everyone feel like a million bucks, or the pastor's great messages. Whatever it is, it is the beginning of the relationship between the guest and your fellowship. At first base is salvation—the decision to follow Jesus Christ. This is where the guest's relating to the church and the church's relating to him or her begins. At second base is discipleship. Now the relationship becomes more of shepherd and flock. Pastors and overseers do intensive care in terms of providing nourishment for everyone. On third base is leadership. Once the person has become a disciple of Jesus Christ, he or she must then be equipped to become a leader in the church. This is never an overnight process, and for some it takes years, but the eventual transition from becoming a follower to becoming a leader is natural for most people. Finally, as the person runs toward home plate again, he or she is ready to reproduce other Christians.

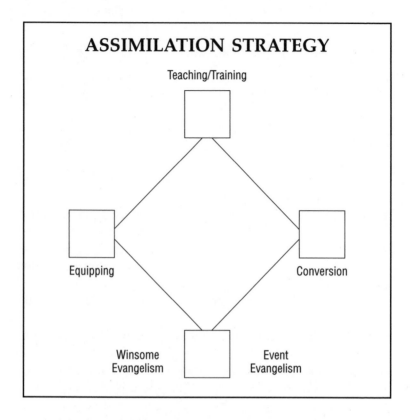

There are some assimilation trends that need emphasis. Just as you once said bulletin and now say worship folder, what used to be a visitor is now a guest. When a shopper goes to Dillard's (department store) at a mall, a sign says, "Welcome! You are our guest." When you go to a Holiday Inn, a sign says, "You are our respected guest. If you need anything, please call." Churches should not run 20 years behind the times. It's time to catch up.

Glen Martin notes other changes. Instead of parking reserved for pastor and staff, now parking spaces are reserved for guests. Instead of home visits, there are phone calls. Instead of introducing visitors, guests retain their anonymity. Instead of back rows for members, there are back rows for guests. Rather than finding friends after the service, we find a guest. Instead of random follow-up, there's an organized tracking system. Instead of assimilation by staff, there is an assimilation team.

CHAPTER 6

TRADITIONAL PASTORAL CARE VS. INTENSIVE CARE

There is no better exercise for strengthening the heart than reaching down and lifting people up.
—*Lawrence B. Hicks*

THE CARING PRINCIPLE

The greatest pastor who has ever lived knew the secret to caring for His people. Before He preached to them, He fed them. Before He ministered to them, He healed them. Before He conversed with them, He gave them something to drink. He knew their conversion was predicated on their well-being, so before He evangelized, He catered.

One of my favorite Bible stories is the calling of Levi, who became Matthew. I particularly enjoy the portrayal of this story in the movie *Jesus of Nazareth*. Jesus had spent the afternoon teaching and healing, to the amazement of all who heard and saw Him. After all, to see a man who had to be lowered through the thatch roof because he had been shriveled since birth get off his pallet and not only walk but dance and shout must have been absolutely glorious. It surely impressed Peter. And it moved a loathed tax collector named Levi as well, who subsequently invited Jesus to share supper with him that evening. Jesus said, "I'd be happy to" (paraphrase), much to the chagrin of the disciples.

Especially Peter, who said something like "You can't be seen dining with sinners. People will think You are no better than they."

Jesus was quick but compassionate in His correction of Peter. "Sinners are precisely the ones I should dine with. A doctor doesn't treat the healthy, but the sick. The Lord is not sent to saints, but to sinners, for the heart of the Lord is mercy" (paraphrase). And with that He entered the house of Levi for supper.

After the eating and the dancing, after the laughing and the partying had subsided, Peter himself was drawn to the door of the tax collector's house to see if his Master had survived, only to find Jesus' arm around Levi, praying with him, transforming him. Peter, too, was drawn in, and in one of the truly magical moments of Scripture, Peter learned what the gospel of Christ was all about. To win souls to the Kingdom, the first step is to become a friend, to accept one another in all our humanity.

That's what pastoral care is all about. It's not just a few moments in the day, but a lifestyle. It's nurturing and committing and loving. But it is never automatic—it is always intentional. In these days the demands of the pastorate are great, and most days there is simply not enough time to do all that needs to be done. "People caring for people" is a plan in which laypersons are trained to assume much of the responsibility once called pastoral care. In it the pastor becomes the facilitator of pastoral care, inverting, if you will, the entire paradigm of congregational expectations.

> **The secret to growing a church is genuine love and concern for people.**
> —Bill Sullivan

How will "People caring for people" work in your church? First, you must train caregivers in at least some of the various needs that are typical to most congregations: grief, divorce, crisis, childbirth, suicide, ministry to the elderly, and so on. You may be fortunate and have some experts in these fields in your congregation, especially if you are near a Christian college campus. But many churches are miles from the closest university and have no such expertise sitting in their pews Sunday after Sunday. Many communities do have Christian counseling centers that are trying to expand their client base (that's what keeps their doors open). Invite some of their counselors to come over and teach your care leaders on Wednesday nights. Most of them will do it free of charge and will be glad to address issues that are particularly evident at your church. Another method is to ask your leaders to direct a book study on one topic of interest so the group can learn together. Training your care leaders means that when they go to a hospital to visit a person facing terminal illness or worrisome surgery, they will be effective as they listen and pray and counsel.

When training caregivers, include the following topics:

Death	Stress
Divorce	Grief
Evangelism	Depression
Unwed Mothers	Assertiveness
Suicide	Aging
Prayer	Relationships/Conflict
Crisis in Childbirth	Encouragement

Each of these subjects can be supported by the many excellent Christian books that have been written to assist today's pastor.

One caution necessary to offer here is that you must be prepared to issue disclaimers when the need arises, for though these caregivers have some initial training in an area, they are not licensed or degreed in any applicable field. Don't allow your caregivers to presume to be professional counselors or to offer "bad" advice. I have avoided misperceptions by publicly calling these people Barnabas ministers because they encourage and lift during times of trouble or trial.

There are two other significant ways that you can do pastoral care. One is through a prayer ministry. One aspect of this ministry is the development of the pastor's prayer partners. Ask individuals in your fellowship to join you in praying on Sunday morning and Sunday night before you share in the worship service. They continue to pray during the service. You may also form a prayer network so that anytime someone is going to the hospital or there is an emergency situation in the church family, within just a matter of minutes every person on the prayer chain is notified and is praying. In a matter of minutes, dozens of people are praying about one concern, lifting the need to the throne of God for His grace and tender mercy. Once you have established this group of prayer partners, you will never want to preach again without them. Additionally, a 24-hour prayer chain that happens once per quarter is a great tool in drawing power from above.

Another very important aspect in pastoral care networking is a phone ministry. This is an excellent opportunity for encouragers to get involved. Besides asking them to contact guests within 24 hours of their visit, assign them lists so that every member of the church is contacted at least once per quarter for prayer requests only. This Phone a Friend ministry can transform gossipers into caring individuals.

When I was pastoring in Nashville at a church of 2,000 members and an even larger extended family, this idea of Phone a Friend seemed like a monumental task. But with methodical scheduling and willing cooperation, we were able to complete it in one quarter. You should have read the notes I received from the first experience. "This is the first time, Pastor, my church has called me in the years I have attended here when they didn't ask me for anything." Now that's pastoral care! One youth pastor in our nation's capital has what he calls a prayer pager for his young people. All the kids are given a code, because most of them have pagers and beepers. They can call their youth pastor at any time, and he has codes from 1 to 99 that cover everything from "I need help with a test tomorrow" to "I need prayer for my relationship with my boyfriend." He doesn't necessarily have to call the individual back unless he or she enters the emergency code, but he has been able to let the youth know with certainty that he cares about their everyday lives.

Why do small groups of laypersons work? A Gallup poll shows that 40 percent of American adults belong to at least one small support group, and 63 percent of those report that they attend a meeting at least twice a month. The findings indicate that 73 percent join in order to grow as persons, 46 percent join because they want a more disciplined spiritual life, 28 percent join for emotional support, and 18 percent join because of personal problems. Members of groups (82 percent) report that their group helps them dispel feelings of loneliness, while 72 percent report receiving encouragement when feeling down. Groups also help people celebrate, handle emotional crises, and make decisions.

Small groups meet needs. Using the second verse of the familiar 23rd psalm as a catalyst, "He makes me lie down in green *pastures*" (emphasis added), one of my former pastoral staff members, David Slamp, developed an acronym that might help you develop a working philosophy of small-group ministry in terms of pastoral care:

Small groups encourage **PERSONAL** involvement. "He . . . gave . . . pastors and teachers, to prepare God's people for works of service" (Eph. 4:11-12).

Small groups encourage caring for **ABSENTEES**. "We who are strong ought to bear with the failings of the weak and not to please ourselves. Each of us should please his neighbor for his good, to build him up" (Rom. 15:1-2).

Small groups enhance **SPIRITUAL** growth. "Instead, speaking the truth in love, we will in all things grow up into him who is the Head, that is, Christ" (Eph. 4:15).

Small groups provide **TRAINING** for service. "He . . . gave . . . pastors and teachers" (Eph. 4:11) for the equipping of the saints.

Small groups facilitate **UNLIMITED** growth. "Until we all reach unity in the faith and in the knowledge of the Son of God and become mature, attaining to the whole measure of the fullness of Christ" (Eph. 4:13).

Small groups aggressively **REACH** the lost. "Go out into the highways and along the hedges, and compel them to come in, that my house may be filled" (Luke 14:23, NASB).

Small groups provide immediate **ENTRY** and acceptance. "Accept one another, then, just as Christ accepted you, in order to bring praise to God" (Rom. 15:7).

And following up on that metaphor is another acronym to help you profile the role of a shepherd. A shepherd . . .

Studies God's Word regularly. "Your word is a lamp to my feet and a light for my path" (Ps. 119:105).

Honors God with holy living, honoring His day, respecting His tithe, obeying His will.

Enables the people to apply God's Word daily, explaining and exposing the truth, exploring the personal meaning.

Prays faithfully for those in his or her care. "We have not ceased to pray for you and to ask that you may be filled with the knowledge of His will in all spiritual wisdom and understanding" (Col. 1:9, NASB).

Helps lead others to Christ, in his or her home and neighborhood.

Equips others to serve, teaching them how, modeling leadership before them, leading them to spiritual maturity.

Represents Jesus to his or her family, friends, and co-workers.

Disciples others to become true Christ-followers. "Go therefore and make disciples of all nations, baptizing them in the name of the Father and the Son and the Holy Spirit" (Matt. 28:19, NASB).

Shepherds should have contagious enthusiasm. Their positive attitude projects that nothing is impossible with God. They should be able to give a clear and direct witness to what Christ has done within their lives, dedicated to living by the Bible and being led by the Spirit and being guided by the mission of the church. Not only should they be filled with the Holy Spirit, but they should fellowship daily with Him as well. Shepherds should not be bogged down in their own problems, but should be free to serve wholeheartedly and effectively, sensitive and committed to others—loving them, caring for them, and ministering to them whenever needed. To these ends, the following "job description" is designed to help each shepherd build the kingdom of God.

SHEPHERD/CAREGIVER JOB DESCRIPTION

1. Make a home visit or phone call to all prospects, group members (upon need) and referrals from the church office.

2. Work with host or hostess to make people in the one-hour weekly group meeting comfortable and relaxed in the home.
3. Talk and pray with the host or hostess before each week's meeting.
4. Report to the pastoral staff each month on the progress of growth.
5. Initiate conversational prayer.
6. Lead the Bible application and discussion.
7. Be responsible for the report of the meeting.
8. Pray at the altar immediately when a member of the group goes forward for prayer in a service.

The ministry of the shepherd in the Sunday School setting is largely one of simply *paying attention*. It involves noticing when those in the class are not as cheerful as usual, not present, not attending to their personal ministries at the church, and so on. Because people are so important, shepherd tasks are people-centered. One of the first things a shepherd does, then, is to build a care list of 8 to 10 Sunday School class members and develop a personal relationship with each one, learning about their families, jobs, and backgrounds. If the shepherd misses them at church, he or she should let them know that early in the week. When there are unusual needs in their lives, the shepherd does what he or she can to meet those needs, at least by letting appropriate people know about it when necessary.

I am convinced that the best way you can do pastoral care is to facilitate it with the laity of your church. But a more hands-on approach you might find productive and effective is the 90-minute-a-day care. In an hour and a half you can minister personally to seven individuals in a way that will not only bless you immensely but also have a great impact on your congregation. The first hour is spent one-on-one with one person in your church or community.

It is 60 minutes of encouraging, building up, and praising. Sometimes this can be done in your office when that is most convenient or comfortable for the individual, but most often, I think, it is wisest to do this outside the church walls. You don't want to spend this precious time conducting church business, so removing yourself from that setting eases the temptation. I have always liked to take a person to a local restaurant for breakfast or lunch, and I always pick up the tab. This casual setting affords opportunity for both light conversation and meaningful dialogue to take place, and if prayer becomes natural, nobody minds. Some care must be given, however, if the person is of the opposite sex and the restaurant is known for ambiance. I normally like to take my wife or a female staff person along in those cases or invite the woman's husband when appropriate. Most people love to have an interested party to listen to them, so refrain from agendas or self-talk as much as possible. This should be that person's time to tell you what is on his or her mind and heart.

Another 15 minutes is spent writing three short notes to three people. I also send birthday cards, anniversary cards, and I invite volunteers (senior adults do perfectly) to come in to address all the cards. When I have had staff members, they also sign the card, and it becomes quite a unique gift in the mail. Unfortunately, when you have handwriting like mine, you have to have your own church card with the church logo so people will know where it came from!

Norman Vincent Peale said some years ago when talking about writing notes, "Christians ought to be in the business of building people up, because there are so many people today already in the demolition business." These notes should be directed by the four Ss: (1) They are sincere, (2) they are short, (3) they are specific, and (4) they are spontaneous.

The final dimension of this 90-minute-a-day care is the 15 minutes spent making three brief phone calls to three people. This is best done, I think, when done systematically. You might want to consider calling each church member on his or her birthday and anniversary, and keep a record of it. A skilled secretary or even a volunteer senior might do this for you by writing down each member's phone number in your pocket calendar on the appropriate day. For example, "Jeff Downs BD, 555-6859." Then, when you turn the page, the phone numbers are there, and all you have to do is call and say, "Hi, Jeff. This is Pastor Goodfella. I wanted to wish you a happy birthday because I love you. I hope you have a great day." If you have no birthday or anniversary calls, then make the calls in alphabetical order, three a day, until you have spoken to every member that year. This opens the door for others in the church to come see them or call them. It's not sacrificing or giving up pastoral care—it's fine-tuning it in order to make it a feasible process without exhausting the pastor.

7

FUND-RAISING VS. GENEROUS BIBLICAL STEWARDSHIP

If you ask for a dollar, you must be willing to give a dollar. A leader must model giving.
—*Melvin Maxwell*

THE GIVING PRINCIPLE

Many churches are desperate to raise their income levels. Have you heard about the following new invention?

New offering plate for churches:

This ingenious invention receives gifts of a dollar or more on a plush cushion with silent graciousness. But when half-dollars are dropped in, it rings a bell; when quarters are given, it blows a whistle; when dimes are slipped in, it fires a shot. But when someone refuses to give, it takes their picture.

—*Stewardship Starters*

There are ways to increase your weekly giving. It is imperative that the people of our churches experience the kind of blessings Jesus describes in Luke 6:38 when He says, "Give, and it will be given to you. A good measure, pressed down, shaken together and running over, will be poured into your lap. For with the measure you use, it will be measured to you." I don't think most people in our church have experienced this kind of "giving living"—the ability to enjoy the privilege of giving and then watch God bring back wonderful blessings into their lives.

A few important lessons will enable you to be an effective leader in this area of ministry. The first one is to plan your offering time each Sunday. Do not go about it in a haphazard manner, but plan what will happen and what is going to be said. Consider the following steps.

First, use the Bible at offering times. It is good for the worship leader to have a meditation from Scripture about giving printed in the worship folder. If you don't have a worship folder or you don't have room in the worship folder you use, you might schedule to have a layperson come to the platform before you pass the plates and read a meditation on giving. (Even a seemingly small matter like semantics, for example, makes a big difference in the tone of the offering. For example, pastors don't *take* the offering—they *receive* it. To use *take* makes it sound as though you're going to steal it to make a payment on your car, and that's certainly not the impression you want to leave. People need to have a sense of purpose and cheerfulness about giving.)

Second, use a "giving witness" at offering time. Someone from your congregation has a testimony about God's graciousness and loving attention in blessing him or her, and most people are happy to share their stories. To God be the glory. One of my flock told the story about the Christmas season he barely had enough money to buy food, much less gifts for his family, and he shared this one night with a few college students he knew. That's when the excitement began. The first thing that happened was an envelope clipped to his office door one morning as he sat inside working. When he discovered it, he opened it to find a $50 bill. Later that week his sister, who had always sent nice but modest gifts at Christmastime, sent a card that year with a check for $50 inside. Soon afterward a blustery wind brought a $10 bill blowing across his front yard. And then came an unexpected cash bonus at his job. Now to some skeptics this may all sound serendipitous, but for most of us it strengthens our faith in the way God works.

Another individual in that same church made a pledge during our expansion program completely on faith, for she had no extra money at the end of her personal budget. Nearly a year later, she testified that *not once* during that year had she had to dip into her normal monthly income to pay her pledge. Every weekly pledge commitment had been met by an outside source of income provided to her by the Lord since that night she had made the pledge.

Third, use a brief personal story of God's blessings. I like to tell the following story: I was a church planter at one time and felt impressed by the Lord to send $50 to some missionaries. When I shared with my wife what had been laid on my heart, we took a look at our checkbook and found $54 in our balance. Not much room for error there. She said, "Honey, I wasn't raised quite like you, but I trust you and have faith in your stewardship commitments. Let's do it." So I wrote the check and sent it to the Carters in Arizona, who were ministering to Native Americans in a small reservation village. Even though I knew it had been the right thing to do, I did begin to wonder how we were going to manage, because at that time in our lives we really never knew when our paychecks were going to be delivered.

The next day I went to the post office, and amazingly I picked up a letter from a student at Asbury Theological Seminary who had been one of my roommates at college. The letter read, "I just had you and Linda on my heart and felt impressed to write you. I'm enclosing a check for you, knowing you will probably put it in the offering plate next Sunday, but it is not for your church. It is for you." And you already know how much it was made out for. Fifty bucks!

Well, as Paul Harvey might say, here's the rest of the story. When the check we sent arrived in Arizona, Doug Carter called immediately. "Stan, your check just arrived. What timing! We had an appointment with the doctor for our daughter, Angie, but we had no money to pay the bill. I was just about to make the dreaded phone call to tell the doctor, but I paused to look at the mail first, and there it was. The Lord was right on schedule, wasn't He?"

How could God touch a poor church planter on the shoulder and say, "Send $50 to missionaries in Arizona," even though He knew the church planter needed it, and at the same time touch a student at Asbury Theological Seminary on the shoulder and say to him, "Send $50 to the Tolers"? A cynical person might ask, "Why didn't God just impress the Asbury student to send his $50 directly to the missionaries in Arizona?" To the first question I say, that's how God works. To the second I suggest that God wanted to pour out His blessings on three families instead of two.

Fourth, use constructive humor at offering time. Have you heard about the preacher who got really desperate for his annual missions offering and went in on the Saturday night before to wire all his pews up to an electrical current? He put a little buzzer up on the platform and decided that on Sunday morning when he said, "Those who will give to the missionary offering, please stand," he would push that button, and they would get a little electrical charge and jump right up to help him. So he got all this scheme ready, and on Sunday morning he said, "I want everybody who will give $100 to world missions please stand." He pushed that button, and people all over the church stood right up. They collected the biggest missionary offering in the history of the church. However, that afternoon he was saddened to learn that six deacons of the church had passed away. Electrocuted.

Once the offering time has been planned, it is important to keep the congregation informed when significant offering achievements take place. Informed givers are happy givers, and if there is a special offering, they will know about it and help the church with a strong personal commitment. As the information is shared, be sure to praise your congregation for their faithfulness in giving; then allow for the entire church fellowship to praise God openly and publicly in any way they want.

It is extremely important to model the spirit of giving from the pulpit, no matter who it is standing behind it, be it a church elder, a deacon, the treasurer, a board member, or the pastor. If he or she asks for a dollar, he or she had better give a dollar. If you ask for $20, you had better have a $20 bill in your hand. In fact, it is wise to have one of the ushers come up to the pulpit to receive the speaker's gift first, not to appear like a Pharisee, but to say to the congregation, "I'm investing in this place because I really believe in what's happening around here."

Your church is full of people with varying interests, not only in the church, but in their involvement in its efforts, so it is wise to realize this and appeal to the different "pockets" of giving. There are those in the *maintenance pocket*, who will always give to the operation of the church —salaries, budgets, materials, and so on. Then there are some who belong to the *brick and mortar pocket*, those who give to buildings, machinery, and so on. There are those in the *missions pocket,* the *benevolence pocket,* the *education pocket,* and the *evangelism pocket.* The whole idea behind these pockets is to remind you that people in the church represent many different backgrounds and emphases, and if you don't open up to these people during the year, then you won't get their participation in stewardship.

Everyone in the church should have a box of numbered offering envelopes handed to them at the end of every fiscal year. These ought to be complimentary in order to make it as easy as possible for people to participate. These envelopes are also important accounting tools and are useful in reporting to the IRS. Every quarter each contributor should receive a record of his or her giving for those three months, and this includes the children. A child who gets in the habit of giving to the church will grow into an adult who finds tithing as natural as paying the mortgage or insurance premium every month. Last year my son got his report in the mail and learned that he had given $96—exactly a tenth of his allowance—and another $100 for missions. He had just returned from a Work and Witness team effort with the youth group, which had really impressed him. Our younger son gave $38.95, plus 15 cents to missions—he has yet to go on a Work and Witness trip. But he'll be going next time! (And I'll guarantee his missions giving will increase.)

There are four reasons to send these personal reports: (1) a person will get his or her giving record, and if there is a question, the bookkeeper's phone number is right on the report; (2) the Sunday following the report distribution is usually a big offering day, because people always seem amazed that they haven't paid as much as they had thought or pledged, and they want to get that amount up to where they had expected it to be; (3) the pastor will want to say a personal thank-you to every giver; and (4) single, individual contributions of $250 or more can no longer be substantiated to the Internal Revenue Service with a canceled check. Donors will not be allowed a tax deduction for an individual cash or property contribution of $250 or more unless they receive a written acknowledgment from the church or charity.

> **When your outgo exceeds your income,**
> **then your upkeep becomes your downfall!**
> **—West Virginia coal miner**

Nothing inspires confidence in a giver like a realistic budget plan. This plan is intentional and well conceived, and you must stick to it in order to earn the respect of your people. But remember that new Christians have to be taught how to give—it's not a natural by-product of salvation. It's too easy to see new people coming into your fellowship and presume that the finances are going to become healthier, but it will take time. The principle is this: financial growth follows people growth. Systematically teach your new people in a discipling class about responsible stewardship, as well as having a stewardship emphasis one month every year.

With apologies to David Letterman, I have my own "Top Ten List":

THE TOP TEN TIPS FOR GOOD CHURCH BUDGETING

Number 10 Build your church budget with your long-term goals and strategic plan in mind.

Number 9 Design your church budget to reflect ministry priorities.

Number 8 Build in a cash reserve equal to an average of one month of church income.

Number 7 Build your church budget based on last year's usable income.

Number 6 Monthly monitor your actual budget performance.

Number 5   Provide monthly financial reports to your church board.

Number 4   Seek church board approval for nonbudget expenditures.

Number 3   Commit to never spend more than 1/12 of your given budget without special approval.

Number 2   Give an annual written report to the congregation.

Number 1   Celebrate by spending excess income on a preapproved capital budget project.

Here are some pointers for Stewardship Month. First, organize a Stewardship Month ministry team. Second, establish a theme. Third, mail letters each week written by members of the ministry action team. On the last week before you start your Stewardship Month, have a special letter sent out, telling the congregation that your church will be in the stewardship series the following Sunday. Remind them that stewardship means more than money or talking about money, and only on the last Sunday of the series will the pastor be talking about giving money and about tithing.

Fourth, present your church budget on that last Sunday, when you speak on giving. Tell them, "I will not preach on giving again this year. This is my one message on giving." Announce the week before that you will be presenting the budget the next week and informing them how their money will be spent, plus how it was spent last year. People are always interested in hearing that. In this final service, ask for a commitment by signing a partnership commitment card with God. It could be in your message outline and printed in the worship folder: "This is between you and God. You can put it in the offering plate if you want to, but I want this to stay in your worship journal all year long so you can see how you are doing throughout the year. Ask everyone to join you in making a commitment to God." It will create a very significant moment as you close out that message on giving.

Finally, it is always important to celebrate the generosity of your people. Let them know what they have done for the kingdom of God. If it is a special-purpose offering, such as for a city rescue mission, take a camera and bring back pictures of improvements made or lives changed. Let them see the faces of those people helped by their giving. If it is a special missions offering, be sure to schedule a missionary speaker during the year who can attest to the usefulness of their generosity. Before you ask your people for another dollar, celebrate their generosity!

❖ **Emphasize giving as an act of worship.**

❖ **Offer workshops on money management and financial planning.**

❖ **Always celebrate the generosity of God's people.**

CHAPTER 8

WORSHIP vs. CELEBRATION

Worship is not performance—it is participation.
—Robert Webber

CELEBRATION PRINCIPLE

Despite the tragic bombing, the overcrowded mass transit system, and the communications breakdowns, I think you'll agree that the 1996 Olympics in Atlanta presented some magnificent moments. I will never forget, for example, the gymnast from Belarussia who had nearly lost his wife a few months before in a car accident, competing for her and her alone. Nor will I forget the sheer power, grace, and speed of Michael Johnson as he ran faster than any other person has ever run. And who can forget the swimmer who gave her medal to her best friend, who was dying of a terrible disease? But one of the most poignant of those 17 days occurred at half-time of the gold medal basketball game between the United States and Yugoslavia.

Whether or not we agree with his religious choices or his political statements, most will agree that Muhammad

Ali was the greatest boxer in the history of the sport. Surveys indicate that he has the most recognized face in the world. In the Rome Olympics of 1960, Ali (then known as Cassius Clay) won a gold medal in the light heavyweight division, but somewhere along the line he lost that medal. When the Olympic Committee learned of this, they decided to replace that medal in an appropriate setting during the '96 Olympics. Millions of us watched as this icon of athletics, trembling under the involuntary force of Parkinson's disease, hobbled to center court for the ceremony, and we remembered. We reminisced. We returned to Rome. We looked at that bloated but still unmarked face; we recalled the moments of his dominance two and three decades ago, the sense of awe and amazement we felt as he "floated like a butterfly and stung like a bee" on his way to winning the world championship an unprecedented three times. We celebrated in our minds and hearts again the Rome Olympics when this brash unknown pummeled the favored Russian boxer into submission and brought the gold medal to America. For 10 minutes in the summer of 1996, we relived the spirit of Rome in 1960.

This is what our worship service ought to have! When we come to church and enter that sanctuary, we are recalling the divine life of God, the Creator of the Universe, who came to earth in the form of a man, who conquered death so that we might have eternal life with Him in Paradise. We need to truly and openly celebrate the most amazing and awesome feat history has ever known. We need to stand as one and commemorate this incredible event as if it were happening again at that very moment—*because it is.*

According to Elmer Towns, 82 percent of our church guests rate worship as the most important reason for joining a church, and I think you'll agree that it is one of the, if not *the,* most important reasons a church exists in the first place. But how can a pastor measure the effectiveness of his or her worship services? One way is to count the number of people involved in the worship leadership. If your church is small and you have a small platform, you may think it's too difficult to include several people in worship. But if you move people on and off the platform, one layperson to lead in prayer, one to read the scripture, another to receive the offering, others to sing solos, you will increase your leadership involvement. When the platform is full of the people, the sanctuary will be full of people. Guaranteed.

When I went to Oklahoma City First Church of the Nazarene in 1984, I said, "We're going to have to expand the platform immediately, because I want more people involved in leading worship." We had only a dozen in the choir, and we needed dozens. At first it seemed like a huge task and a grandiose dream, but that platform has been remodeled three times since then to seat a choir of 50 and an orchestra of 20, and that church has grown from approximately 200 to high attendance days of 1,300. As a matter of fact, they are currently under a building program to expand the sanctuary to seat 1,300.

If your church is small, you may feel that you have to do everything, but one secret to growth is to decrease the number of things you do every Sunday. I knew of a pastor who drove the church bus, led the congregational singing, taught the adult Sunday School class, made all the announcements from the pulpit, led the congregational prayer, and sang solos—not to mention preached the sermon and pronounced the benediction. And his wife played the piano. They did *everything*. Even drove everyone home on the church bus after services. People applauded their energy and commitment, but nobody got involved in worship because they were never expected to. (*I* was that pastor.) I know that initially you must do some of that out of necessity, but there comes a time, no matter how big or small a church is, when you need to realize that if you do too much, you will die from overexposure and your laypeople will stagnate from underexposure. Stand behind the pulpit only when what you have to say really counts. Have a layperson make the announcements—and don't have him or her read the bulletin—that might seem demeaning to your congregation. Ask a lay leader to pray the congregational prayer. Allow a board member to receive the offering. And by all means, if you sing like me, don't insist on a weekly solo.

> **Pastor, don't make the announcements. You'll die from overexposure!**
>
> **—Stan Toler**

Another way to measure the effectiveness of worship seems obvious: count the number of people sitting in the pews. If you have empty pews everywhere, then it may indicate you need to do something different, to get a new look in the sanctuary. This is particularly important if your attendance was once much larger than it is today and there are only 50 people sitting in a sanctuary built for 300. One such church in California has removed (temporarily, they hope) the last three or four pews on each side of the sanctuary. Second, they have agreed to sit on one side of the middle aisle, and the pastor has gone from a sizable pulpit on the platform to a more modest, mobile podium that he places on floor level in the front of that one side. Now to some that may sound like they have admitted defeat, but I contend that if a church is going to grow, it needs to make those who do attend more comfortable by bringing them closer together. Hey—if no one is coming anyway, there's nothing to lose by making a change.

Do your people invite their friends and neighbors to come to church? If they don't, then you have to do something about making worship a positive, uplifting experience. One pastor learned the hard way that no one wanted to come to church because he was always making them feel guilty, telling them everything they were doing wrong, preaching about their sinful nature. Who wants to hear that *every Sunday*, week in and week out?

It is important to know what your people are thinking, to hear from the men and women who shake your hand every Sunday. Sure, there will always be the one person who will come by after the service and really blast you on what you're doing wrong, but it's usually best to ignore him or her. The majority of comments will be constructive, and it really helps to listen to what your people have to say. You might consider mailing out a survey to find out what the congregation thinks, even mailing it to the community in general. If you find out the idiosyncrasies of the people in your church and community, you will be able to deal with those things effectively and assimilate them into your worship experience. It always strengthens the worship service when you listen to your people.

A worship service that is dynamic, that celebrates the life of Christ and promotes the lifestyle of the Christian, will be an attraction few can ignore. The world has music, for instance, that is upbeat and moving forward. It may not always be positive in its message, but it certainly has some type of "pick-me-up" in it. Some part of your service deserves that kind of "lifter," spiritually speaking, something that will make people want to clap their hands and tap their feet. That is not to suggest moving to a completely contemporary praise service, discarding the great hymns of the Church, but it is important to mix the tempo of the music and service so it will have interest to a broader base of people.

That's why it is so imperative to build a worship team, a group of people who meet regularly, who know something about worship, who are in tune with the Spirit and can sit down and talk about it. It involves your musical people and the pastoral team. Most pastors can learn how to lead worship services better, despite all the classes they have had at seminary or Bible college. One reason churches don't have a sense of celebration is that they don't *plan* for any celebration. The worship team can be an immense help in this area—from the praise singers on the platform to the choices of hymns and praise choruses, even to choosing the people who will lead the various aspects of worship.

If you are looking at praise songs in a traditional church, do your best to blend them in. On the other hand, if you have a church that loves hymns but you are trying to reach the baby boomers and baby busters of your community, you might start an optional service that would have praise songs in it—a more contemporary sound. Christ Church in Brentwood, Tennessee, has three different types of services each Sunday. They offer a liturgical-type service, in which they serve Communion every Sunday in order to reach a lot of mainliners and Catholics in their community. The sermon is pure gospel, and the pastor wears a robe. Then they have a service during which they blend the hymns and praise songs. In the third service the choir director is everywhere—in the back of the sanctuary, in the balcony, down the aisles, and people are jumping and shouting and and all sorts of things! Somehow they have learned to mesh all this, and they are reaching a vast number of people, winning them to the Kingdom.

Each service ought to have a theme in mind. If you had been pastoring in Atlanta during the Olympics, you might have planned a service dealing with victory, with running the race. After the bombing you might have wanted a theme about fear, planning every song and aspect of worship to deliver your people from all those anxieties and worries they had. Even if you plan your sermons a year in advance or a quarter in advance, it helps your worship leaders a great deal in terms of deciding what needs to happen thematically in that worship experience.

But no amount of planning, no amount of singing, no amount of changing will work if you don't build all of it on the throne of God, kneeling in prayer and asking for His guidance. For me, if I don't have prayer partners, I don't preach. I have to have people who will pray with me and for me. About 25 years ago John Maxwell and I began praying every Saturday night and Sunday morning in the sanctuary. We walked in and out of every aisle, every pew, praying for the presence of God in that service. Later each Sunday morning, prayer partners joined us, walking up and down the hallways and into Sunday School class-rooms, praying for the teachers. We did this because we were old-fashioned enough to believe that when God visits our worship services, something marvelous is going to happen beyond our greatest dreams or expectations.

Much of what happens in worship is predicated on the sermon, so spending ample quality time in sermon preparation is vitally important. Never forget your source of authority. It was Billy Graham who said many years ago and continues to say today whenever he preaches, "The Bible says . . ." We need to understand that our authority does not come from our degrees posted on the wall or our title posted on our door; our authority comes from above. Not long ago during a credential committee meeting a man came seeking ordination. As he interviewed, there was a great deal of discussion about whether this man should be ordained or not, and it came to the point at which someone on the committee asked him, "How would you feel if we did not ordain you this year?"

The man looked the committee members in the eye and said, "Brothers, that would be all right. God has al-ready ordained me, and He's just waiting on you boys to get the paperwork done."

You've ever dreamed you were preaching only to awaken and discover you were.

Used with permission,
Stan Toler and Mark Hollingsworth,
"You Might Be a Preacher If . . ."
(Tulsa, Okla.: Albury Press, 1996).

Remember why you preach. You're not teaching for instruction; you're preaching for decision. It is not your calling only to build up the believers in the faith and to feed them spiritually, but you are also called to win the lost for Christ. Paul summarized his ministry in the 15th chapter of Romans by saying that he had a ministry not only to the saved but also to the unsaved and that he needed to give a moment for people to come to know the Lord. Many pastors have abandoned invitation times, the challenge to accept

Christ as a personal Savior, but these are a tremendous way to measure the effectiveness of the worship service, by challenging the people to respond to what is being presented.

It is important for you to know your congregation. Do you have a group of senior citizens to whom you are speaking? Then think about what should be said to them. Is your crowd full of teenagers? What do they need to hear to survive the turmoils of growing up these days? One church started a Saturday night service for baby busters. The whole design for that service was quite different from anything they had ever experienced: they had done surveys and discovered that they wanted about 10 minutes of preaching, then a break for snacks, then a discussion about the sermon in the sanctuary, with soft drinks and coffee. And then they had a dramatic presentation or a Christian video. Their purpose was to present what the world was saying about God, or what Hollywood has to say about God, knowing that we all learn about God in different ways by various methods. It all has to do with audience.

As you prepare your messages, ask yourself these eight questions, as Rick Warren suggests:
1. To whom will I be preaching?
2. What does the Bible say about their need?
3. What is the most practical way to say it?
4. What is the most positive way to say it?
5. What is the most encouraging way to say it?
6. What is the simplest way to say it?
7. What is the most personal way to say it?
8. What is the most interesting way to say it?

I recently attended a service at a large Presbyterian church that communicates visually as well as orally. They have a wonderful worship folder, inside of which are the pastor's sermon notes. It is three-hole punched so the people can take it home and put it into their spiritual journals. I went to another church on the cutting edge of technology.

They had a screen on either side of the platform, and as the pastor made his points, those points came up on the screen for everyone to read. It was quite effective in retaining the thrust of the message.

Speaking of messages, the best message is a brief message. The late George Burns once quipped, "A good sermon should have a good beginning and a good ending, and they should be as close together as possible." Some of you are preaching absolutely too long! A few years ago I went to the 30 fastest-growing churches in America, and I put a stopwatch on every preacher. The average sermon was 25 minutes long, many of them much shorter. If you want to reach the younger generation, particularly, then you have only a 30-minute time span in which to do it. They check out after that amount of time because, like it or not, they were raised with a television schedule that is built in 30-minute increments. It's the same way with Sunday School lessons, so let your teachers know what every elementary and secondary school teacher already knows—30 minutes and they're out!

The key to better preaching is not long harangues; no, the key to better preaching is better research. Most ministers know how to outline and do a pretty good job organizing, because they have been taught in schools and in religion departments to have good homiletics and hermeneutics. However, too frequently they forget to put *substance* into their style. Begin to build a file of resources to which you can go and find notes and articles on any topic, from grace to mercy to justice. Block out time in your schedule to go to the local public or university library to read up on current issues, trends, discoveries, and movements. Don't rely on the same five sources you've always used. If you want your churches to grow, then you, personally, must grow. Listen to great preaching, and model yourself after that. Read books voraciously. Use computer technology. Subscribe to good periodicals.

A second key to more effective preaching is the use of humor. *Dallas Morning News* researcher Anne Belli Gesalman reported in the August 3, 1996, edition her discovery that if a pastor wants the flock to move up to the front and carefully listen to the message, the pastor should pepper his or her preaching with a pinch of humor. For some it comes more naturally than for others, but as one church leader in Dallas said, "Much of what we're about as people of faith is discovering the joy of our relationships to God and each other, and I think humor is an important dimension of who we are as human beings."

Francis of Assisi said, "Do you want to know one of the best ways to win over people and lead them to God? It consists of giving them joy and making them happy."

Pope John Paul II said, "Christ came to bring joy: joy to children, joy to parents, joy to families and to friends, joy to workers and to scholars, joy to the sick and joy to the elderly, joy to all humanity. In a true sense, joy is the keynote of the Christian message and the recurring motif of the church."

Billy Graham joins in that spirit: "People go to a football game today and shout their heads off, or go to a circus and cheer act after act. They become enthusiastic about everything conceivable, but when it comes to spiritual matters they think we are supposed to become sober and wear black, and never have a good time or enjoy a religious event."

Circus founder P. T. Barnum wrote, "Men, women and children who cannot live on gravity alone need something to satisfy their lighter moods and hours, and he who ministers to this want is in a business established by the author of our nature. If he worthily fulfills his mission and amuses without corrupting, he need never feel that he has lived in vain."

Martin Luther suggested, "If you're not allowed to laugh in heaven, I don't want to go there."

German theologian Dietrich Bonhoeffer wrote, "God cannot endure that unfestive, mirthless attitude of ours in which we eat our bread in sorrow, with pretentious, busy haste, or even with shame. Through our daily meals he is calling us to rejoice, to keep holiday in the midst of our working day."

John Holbert, professor of preaching at Southern Methodist University's Perkins School of Theology, pointed out that there is biblical precedent for the use of humor in worship, beginning with the Book of Genesis and the story of Adam and Eve wearing fig leaves. "Fig leaves feel like sandpaper," he said, chuckling. He said he recently delivered what he thought was a very powerful message, interjected with humor, when he was a guest speaker in Washington, D.C. He framed his sermon around this story of Adam and Eve, but no one in the congregation smiled, much less laughed out loud. This was a first for him. Afterward, one of the church members told him that he enjoyed the sermon so much he almost laughed.

"Why didn't you?" Holbert asked.

"Oh," the man replied, "we don't laugh here."

Holbert suggests that "society as a whole has become darker in its humor. But I hope that churches could use humor as a way of looking at themselves honestly, to build up the community."

A third key is to plan your preaching schedule to include special seasons. Within the Evangelical church especially, there seems to be an appalling lack of interest in this area. If we say we believe in Holy Spirit power, then why don't we celebrate Pentecost? If we really believe in the Advent, then why don't we teach people that Advent is a season of waiting and anticipation? Christmas is the season of joy. Epiphany is the season for evangelism and mission. It is important that we have that kind of form and develop that kind of interest in our churches. People enjoy the seasons, and they enjoy listening to sermons that remind them why Jesus came. In the season of Lent, they love to think introspectively about Christ's suffering, about His sacrifice on the Cross, and His joyous resurrection. Lent is the season of spiritual renewal. Holy Week is the season to enter into the major events of our salvation. Easter is the season to celebrate the power of Christ to overcome evil. People enjoy the celebration of rituals, and these are important celebrations to the church, so your sermons should be strategically planned accordingly.

LYLE SCHALLER ASKS 3 QUESTIONS ABOUT WORSHIP

1. Today I found this worship service to be
   ___ a joyful, meaningful, uplifting, and/or helpful experience
   ___ a dull, lifeless, and comparatively uninspiring experience
   ___ somewhere in between those two

2. Today the sermon
   ___ spoke directly to the concerns and questions I brought with me
   ___ was interesting, but not especially relevant to me
   ___ was neither interesting nor very helpful

3. The most meaningful and helpful part of today's worship experience for me was (please check only one)
   ___ congregational singing
   ___ prayers
   ___ sermon
   ___ confessions
   ___ anthem or special music
   ___ being a part of this worshiping community
   ___ simply the chance to be here to worship God
   ___ Holy Communion
   ___ the familiar liturgy

151

Then seek to involve your people in a personal response to what is presented. In the book *Could You Not Tarry One Hour?* Larry Lea discusses praying the Lord's Prayer with its various lines. It will revolutionize your prayer life. One of the lines in which we ask God to "forgive us our trespasses as we forgive those who trespass against us" calls for us to look to God and say, "I am going to turn some things over to You today." The author suggests that at that moment "you should cup your hands with me. We have a lot of fears, and these fears are too great for me. I cannot handle them myself. All my anxieties and fears and frustrations and my pain, my financial needs, my sickness, whatever it is, I am placing this in your hands before God." He goes on to say, "Let's don't nurse it; let's don't curse it; let's don't rehearse it, but let's give it to God."

At this point he says, "We are going to give this to God, so turn your hands over and let go of it." With that we say, "God, it's Yours. I let go of it."

Now, I'm not trying to make you raise one hand or two, or trying to make you say "Amen!" or anything else. What I do want you to do in worship is to bring people to a sense of response to what has been presented, so that when the songs have been sung, when the prayers have been prayed, when the message has been delivered, people will walk out of the sanctuary saying, "Praise God. He was in this place today, speaking and listening to my heart."